The Modern Bowhunter
—
Geared Up!

The Modern Bowhunter
Geared Up!

By Curt Wells

Expert Advice from the
Equipment Editor of
"The Number One Bowhunting Magazine"

Bowhunter Magazine Series . . .
The Modern Bowhunter—Geared Up!

Publisher *Jeffrey S. Waring*
Editor *Dwight Schuh*
Art Director *Mark Olszewski*
Assistant Editor *Brian Fortenbaugh*
Associate Editor *Lori James*
Editorial Assistant *Sally Burkey*
Cover Design & Book Layout *David J. Siegfried*

Acknowledgments

All photos: Curt Wells
Illustration page 83: David J. Siegfried

First Edition
Library of Congress Cataloging-in-Publication Data
ISBN: 1-934622-97-4

Dedication

Patti.

No other word in my first book could possibly precede the name of my wife of 35 years. We started our life together as young kids and raised two outstanding sons, Jason and Jared. Patti's tolerance, patience, understanding, and support have risen above and beyond what any outdoorsman could expect from a spouse. I am the person I am because of my loving wife. This book, indeed my life, would not have been possible without her.

Patti is not alone in her support. My parents, Joan and Verne, molded me as a person. Mom taught me to set goals and pursue them with vigor. Dad didn't hunt but introduced me to the outdoors through years of taking my brother, Dave, and me fishing. Both are gone now but never forgotten . . .

I'd also like to recognize three other people who bear some responsibility for my being wherever it is that I am as an outdoor writer and bowhunter.

In the mid-80s, M.R. James, founder of Bowhunter Magazine, recognized something in a struggling writer and encouraged me in many ways. Advice and instruction, through detailed personal letters, were treasures of constructive criticism only a writer appreciates.

Dwight Schuh, Bowhunter editor, has gone out of his way, for reasons I still don't understand, to include me in the magazine, first as a freelancer, then contributor, then as equipment editor. He too, has taken time to mentor me, and if only a smidgen of his considerable writing skills have rubbed off, I am grateful.

Then there's Jeff Waring, Bowhunter Magazine's publisher. Jeff is one of those people you love to work for. He's always made me feel like a member of the team, and I'd walk through fire if Jeff needed me to. Jeff is both a dedicated professional and, like M.R. and Dwight, a friend I'm proud to claim.

Of course, there are other people who influenced me along the way. Rodney Harris, a good 'ol boy from Missouri, was the first to take me hunting back in 1970 when we were teenage Air Force brats in Upper Michigan. English teachers, editors, hunting buddies who helped with photographs, guides, outfitters, and many others contributed to my growth as a bowhunting writer, and I appreciate them all, more than they'll ever know.

Contents

Foreward
By Dwight Schuh, Bowhunter Editor

For several years before signing on full time with Bowhunter Magazine, I read Curt Wells' stories in the magazine. Then, when I officially assumed the role as Editor in 1997, I started reading and editing Curt's raw manuscripts. One thing that always struck me was the parallel between his way of looking at bowhunting and mine. "This guy thinks just the way I do," I mused. Whether that makes us both brilliant or both fools is open to debate. One way or the other, we do seem to be kindred spirits, which is to say I can relate to what Curt says and writes. And virtually without exception, I find his approach to bowhunting right on. There is nothing phony about Curt Wells. Consistent with the name of his regular column in Bowhunter, he is "Tried and True."

One thing that has always drawn me to Curt and his writing is his commitment to the bow and arrow. Some writers dabble at bowhunting, but they're quick to pick up a firearm if that seems the most expedient way to get a story. Not so Curt. He is a bowhunter, through and through, and he's committed to hunting with a bow — or not at all.

And he invests himself in every hunt. He does his homework, gets in shape, researches gear, hones his archery skills, and puts in his time. His high degree of success is no accident. He earns it.

As we planned our first major hunt together, an excursion for moose in Alaska, I was impressed with Curt's initiative in helping lead the charge. Even though I had initiated the hunt, Curt immediately said, "What can I do to help?", and without prompting he was on the phone and Internet, ordering maps, securing needed gear, gathering information. He demonstrated not only initiative but also knowledge in engineering a successful hunt.

Curt has been involved with Bowhunter Magazine TV from the very beginning. Because of his knowledge and skill with equipment, Publisher Jeff Waring and I did not hesitate to tab him as co-host of Tech Talk, a segment on gear and equipment, alongside Group Publisher Mike Carney. Not at all incidentally, Curt has appeared in many of the TV program's feature segments — probably more than any other individual — because when he goes to the field, he gets the job done.

Having bowhunted across North America, and literally around the world with successful trips to Africa and New Zealand, Curt has mastered all styles of gear related to bowhunting. And, as Equipment Editor for Bowhunter Magazine, he has personally set up and tested thousands of equipment items from arrow rests to Zebra strings. He knows not only bowhunting but also bowhunting equipment. That's why you can trust Curt Wells in **Geared Up!** to help you gear up for a lifetime of successful bowhunting.

Introduction

It's safe to say, no other type of hunting is more "equipment intensive" than bowhunting. The quantity and diversity of gear a bowhunter needs, particularly one who hunts a variety of game and habitats, is staggering. It can also be intimidating to the beginner. The novice must understand it takes years to accumulate the range of gear experienced bowhunters have stashed in their garages, sheds, and closets. For some, collecting all that gear is part of the fun.

Like anglers, serious bowhunters will try just about any product they believe can give them an edge when it comes to taking a good buck, bull, gobbler, or even a fat doe. Some products will increase your odds of success, some will make you more comfortable, and some can make bowhunting more fun. Others are gimmicks that quietly fade away. The bowhunting consumer is intelligent enough to sort out which is which and won't spend his hard-earned money on junk.

Experience is our greatest educator, but a good bowhunter is never satisfied with what he knows. He constantly asks questions about the animals he hunts and the gear he uses. Why does one particular piece of gear work better than another? Could something be done to improve a product? He's a problem solver, whether that involves a difficult stalk or an equipment issue.

Over 27 years of bowhunting, I've always been one to examine or test a product with an analytical yet critical eye. I appreciate engineering done in the field rather than the office, and the difference is far more readily apparent than some manufacturers believe. Poor engineering is a pet peeve of mine, especially when the solution to a problem is so obvious. Sorry, don't get me started on engineers . . .

In the following chapters we'll examine nearly every imaginable aspect of bowhunting equipment. I certainly don't have all the answers or know all the tricks. This book is intended to make you think about your bowhunting equipment, give you some ideas, and maybe spark a few of your own.

I'm a bowhunter first and foremost, so we're going to approach everything from a bowhunter's point of view. Throughout this book you'll also read practical advice for the bowhunter offered in both hunting stories and Quick Tips. Because there's so much ground to cover, we won't deal with a lot of intricate technical details or delve too deeply into the process of tuning bows and arrows. We won't be covering competitive archery or the camping gear you might need on a bivouac hunt for sheep either. Someone else can, and has, tackled those topics.

You'll also see specific products mentioned in this book. Because I am the equipment editor at Bowhunter Magazine, I must maintain objectivity. Consequently, I am not on any company's pro-staff, nor am I paid by any company to promote their products. In some cases I mention products as examples of certain types of gear or to illustrate references to specific features. Others are mentioned because I've found them to be useful in the field and of high quality. Are there other similar products of equal quality? Of course. But I can't possibly use every bow, pack, or pair of boots on the market. The archery/bowhunting market is in a constant state of flux with new products emerging daily. Use my suggestions for reference, then apply your own judgment and budget. Contact information for all manufacturers is listed in the back of the book, page 206.

It's my sincere hope that when you close this book you'll have picked up a few things that'll make your bowhunting life easier, more efficient, and ultimately, more fun.

Fun — that's really what we're all here for, isn't it?

CHAPTER ONE

When my new high-tech bow wasn't performing, I pulled out my old standby, a Martin Cougar Magnum, and took this nice Montana bull elk. The bow doesn't make the bowhunter.

Choosing A Bow

Years ago, after setting up elk camp in Montana's Crazy Mountains, I ran into a problem. I was shooting some practice arrows with my Golden Eagle Vision, one of the fastest bows of the day, and something wasn't right. I'd had my bow shooting perfectly back home in North Dakota but always ran into arrow flight problems when hunting high altitude. Every September, the solution was the same — turn down the spring pressure on my Berger Button, a common arrow rest component "back in the day."

That wasn't working with my Golden Eagle. Frustrated, and anxious to get hunting, I put the Vision away and pulled out my back-up bow, a green-speckled 80-lb. Martin Cougar Magnum with limbs as thick as canoe paddles. It was a killer bow, with which I'd taken a number of bull elk, deer, and antelope, so we were buddies.

It was a comparatively slow bow but very forgiving. I had complete confidence in my old friend, and by hunt's end we had combined to send a Zwickey-tipped arrow into the heart of a beautiful 6x6 bull elk. The flight of that arrow is a life-long memory.

The very next spring I converted to a Black Widow recurve bow and cedar arrows. That fall I killed a bull elk, a decent muley buck, and a pronghorn.

Now skip forward, over many hunts in several countries, to 2007. From spring through fall I killed ten animals using five different bows, various arrows, broadheads and accessories.

I apologize if that sounds like chest-thumping, but here's my point. The bow does not make the bowhunter. A bow is simply a means of delivering an arrow. Becoming a bowhunter means studying game, habitat, and striving to see how close you can get to your quarry. The bow and the arrow simply help you to consummate the hunt.

The animals you hunt do not care what bow you use or how much money you spent on it. I do not care; other bowhunters shouldn't either. A good bowhunter will take game with any bow you put in his hands.

Still, it's the number one question I hear: "Which is the best bow to buy?"

It sounds like a dodge, but there truly is no correct answer.

For the most part, rifles and shotguns fit anyone. Bows do not. They're personal hunting tools that must be fitted to your body and shooting style. Ten archers can shoot the same bow and come away with ten opinions. Only you know which bow "feels" best in your hands. That doesn't mean you go into the process blind.

The standard advice is to visit an archery pro shop, but that's not always possible, and some pro shops, particularly in big-box stores, have young employees with little experience. Or they have an agenda, steering customers in biased directions toward the equipment they must sell. Quality pro shops offer expert help and won't steer you wrong.

In an attempt to clear up some confusion and send you into that pro shop with some rudimentary knowledge of what you're up against, consider the following advice. You may encounter conflicting opinions, but my purpose is to give you a head start in your research and in the decision-making process. You'll still need hands-on experience, whether you're looking for your first bow or your tenth.

Since we're gearing up the "modern" bowhunter on these pages, I won't spend many words addressing traditional bows such as recurves and long-bows. Traditional bowhunters may not find these first four chapters useful, but after that this book will apply to all bowhunters, regardless of weapon choice.

That said, here are some thoughts on traditional archery that may help you decide if it's for you.

Traditional archery is fun, exhilarating and romantic. It is also challenging, time-consuming, and difficult. It's worth the effort, but be prepared to shoot many hours building calluses on your fingers, muscles in your back and shoulders, and committing the trajectory of your arrow to memory.

Today's recurves and longbows are often technological marvels, built with high-tech laminations and resins, and the risers are sometimes machined from aluminum or wood. Longbows are more primitive than recurves, thus arrow speeds are generally slower, and the bows are a bit more difficult to shoot.

Length is a primary question when choosing a traditional bow. Like all bows, going to extremes is usually a bad idea. Bows can range from 55" to 65" plus. Longer archers should use longer bows because of finger pinch.

Most tend to "overbow" themselves with too much draw weight. Few archers can comfortably shoot a 70-lb. traditional bow, and even 60 lbs. may be more than most can handle. The experienced traditional bowhunters I know shoot draw weights somewhere in the 50s. It's all about control, and a comfortable draw weight will contribute to better shooting form and accuracy. A heavy arrow/broadhead combination in the 500- to 700-grain range will help maintain sufficient kinetic energy with slower traditional bows.

Other decisions include grip style or whether you'll shoot off the shelf or an elevated rest. When I shot traditional, I preferred shooting off the shelf because it put the arrow closer to my hand, helping with my instinctive shooting skills.

Some excellent recurves and longbows are available "off the shelf," or you may opt for a custom-made traditional bow that'll cost you serious money. If your mind is made up to go traditional, I suggest you seek the advice of an experienced traditional archer, purchase books on the subject, or visit traditional websites such as the Leatherwall at www.bowsite.com.

THE BASICS

Throughout this book we'll be focusing only on bowhunting, not competitive archery, but as a bowhunter your basic needs are similar — a bow that offers a blend of forgiveness, consistency, and speed.

If you seek the perfect bow, you'll be looking a long time. It doesn't exist. Look for the bow that's right for you!

Forgiveness is number one, because when hunting you can't always employ perfect shooting form. Shooting straight down from a tree-stand, or from your knees, leaning around a stump and under a deadfall, are real-life hunting situations that don't lend themselves to perfect shooting form. Minor mistakes in technique should not result in a significant change of your arrow's point of impact at reasonable hunting yardages. That is the definition of forgiveness.

Consistency is next, and that comes with practice and building familiarity with your equipment. The act of shooting an arrow needs to become automatic. Consistent practice creates a consistent archer.

Last comes arrow speed. Ultra-fast bows generally require excellent shooting form. The price you pay for a fast arrow often is a loss of some degree of forgiveness. As with almost anything in life, avoiding the extremes is good advice. Here are a few more questions you'll need to answer.

Will you shoot a right-handed bow or left? This may seem a strange question but it's not, especially for the beginner. Not everyone has a dominant eye (myself, for example), but most do, and you need to find out which is yours. Try this simple test. With both eyes open, pick a small object, like a light switch at the other end of the room, then extend your arm and put your thumb over that object. Now, close your left eye. If your thumb is still over the object, you're right-eye dominant. If your thumb has moved off the object, open your left eye and close your right. If your thumb moves back over the object, you're left-eye dominant.

If you're right-eye dominant, you should shoot a right-handed bow, and vice versa. Even if you've been right-handed all your life, but you're left-eye dominant, you might consider shooting a left-handed bow. Starting out that way is much easier than converting later. You can still shoot right-handed with left-eye dominance, but you'll have to close your left eye when aiming. Though I don't have a dominant eye, I've always closed my left eye when aiming.

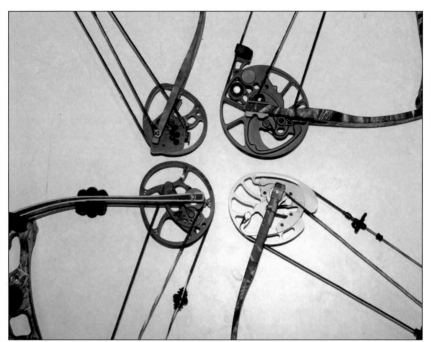

Cam design determines how a bow feels as you draw and shoot. There are four basic designs. Clockwise from top left, dual-cam, single-cam, Binary cam and hybrid or cam-and-½.

Which cam — dual, single, hybrid, or binary? This is a significant question, and it can get overly technical, particularly if a beginner attempts to understand the differences. There are trade-offs in each system, and none is perfect.

Dual cams generally create a faster bow, as each limb is loaded by a cam. Depending on the design of the cams, these bows can have a force-draw curve ranging from ultra-smooth with a soft wall (the feel at full draw), to rough and radical with a hard wall. The smooth, soft designs tend to be slower than the hard-drawing cams. The negative of the dual-cam bow is the necessity to keep the cams in synchronization. Both cams must roll over at the exact same moment in the draw and subsequent release. String and cable creep can cause that synchronization to go out of whack, which will affect the accuracy and consistency of your bow. Dual-cam bows tend to be a bit noisy as well.

Single-cam bows are very popular because you don't have to worry about cam synchronization; therefore, they're easier to tune and will stay tuned longer. Also, the newest technology has addressed the problems of less-than-straight-and-level nock travel inherent in early single-cam bows. Single cams are smooth, quiet, and relatively shock-free, but all things being equal, are typically the slowest of the three designs. The differences are negligible, and technology is narrowing the gap.

Hybrid cams, invented by Darton Archery, are sort of a cross between the dual and single. The lower "power" cam does the loading of the limbs while the upper "control" cam acts more like an idler wheel. A slave cable between the two cams is designed to ensure the cams stay in synchronization. A hybrid-cam system approaches the speed of a dual cam, and the consistency of the single-cam design. It is not immune to synchronization problems, but keeping the bow in tune is much easier than on a dual cam.

Binary cams, made popular by BowTech Archery, are modified twin-cams that are slaved to each other rather than to the bow's limbs. This eliminates the split harness present on other designs, and because the cams tend to equalize each other, there are no synchronization problems. This design also creates a very fast bow, so it's becoming quite popular.

In the end, the shape of a bow's force-draw curve, a graph that illustrates power stroke, is probably the number one factor in what sort of impression a bow gives a potential buyer. Cam design determines the "feel" of a bow as you draw. If the bow draws smoothly with no humps or bumps, then falls into the valley with ease, it's generally pleasing to the archer. It also means less energy is being stored and the bow will likely shoot a slower arrow. Fast bows tend to have rude draw cycles that build to a peak of stored energy, then fall off quickly, often with a jerk going into the valley. Other cam designs fall somewhere in between.

It's a personal thing. To some, a "rude" draw cycle is a fair trade off for arrow speed, even though such bows are less forgiving. Others prefer the smooth, easy draw and consistent accuracy. For them, speed isn't a factor. And two archers can draw the same rough-drawing bow and come away with opposing impressions. Personally, I don't like a bow that has a radical "break over," because it can cause a jerk hard enough to pop an arrow off the rest. You can get used to such a draw cycle, but for novice bowhunters I'd suggest a smoother-drawing bow.

Long or short? Okay, you've chosen right or left hand and the cam system you want, now what about axle-to-axle length? At the risk of oversimplification, short bows are a bit more difficult to shoot and less consistent in accuracy than longer bows. Short bows are easier to maneuver around in a treestand or ground blind, but the severe string angle at full draw will put a peep sight further away from your eye. Your grip and release become more critical with short bows, and if you go too short the arrows in a bow quiver may extend below the bottom cam, exposing nocks to damage.

Longer bows tend to have a smoother draw cycle and are usually quieter and more forgiving to shoot. If they're too long they can be awkward in some situations.

Your draw length also factors in here. If you have a particularly short draw length, say 27 inches, you can more easily shoot a 32-inch bow. If your draw length is 31 inches, you may want to stick to bows at least 34 to 36 inches long, or longer.

If you're one of the few bowhunters who still shoot compound bows with fingers, you'll definitely need a longer bow to reduce finger pinch. Depending on your draw length, and how many fingers you use, you may need a bow in the 38 to 40-inch range.

Draw length? This is a good time to talk about draw length, the most crucial measurement of all. In the past, draw length was measured with the archer all stretched out, upright at full draw with bow arm extended and elbow locked. I used to shoot a 32-inch draw length 20 years ago. Although I haven't shrunk (I'm still 6'5"), I now shoot 30 inches.

The locked-out elbow method was fine as long as you were always shooting in an upright position. In odd shooting positions, accuracy suffered. More problems occurred when archers over-rotated their elbows and their arms would get abused by the string. Heavy clothing was always getting in the way of the bowstring. Having your body all stretched out just isn't efficient.

The solution came with the advent of cam designs that allowed archers to draw to a solid "wall" rather than settling inconsistently into a soft valley at full draw. Once we could draw to the stop and hold tight, it was more effective to shorten the draw length and shoot with a bent elbow. This served several purposes. Consistency improved because there was no valley "bottom" to locate. Just take it to the wall and hold it there.

A bent elbow also keeps your arm out of the way to the point where arm guards are not necessary for some, and heavy sleeves are less of a problem.

More importantly, shooting with a slightly bent elbow, which requires a bit more strength, ensures you come to full and complete draw, hard against the wall, no matter what contortions your body is going through. It keeps your draw consistent in length and your elbow also acts as a shock absorber, soaking up the hand shock of the bow's release.

Your anchor point will be a factor in determining correct draw length. Finger shooters tend to put the tip of their index finger in the corner of their mouth. Release shooters generally anchor lower with their jawbone settled into the crease between the thumb and forefinger. Different release designs can alter your hand position, so you'll just have to find what's comfortable for you. I've always anchored so the bowstring just touches the end of my nose. That gives me another point of reference to go along with my anchor and a peep sight (Chapter 4).

Once you've found your anchor, you can get measured for draw length. This is not as simple as it sounds, so have it done by someone who knows what he is doing. The best method uses a lightweight bow, with no cam or valley, that

Determining correct draw length is critical. For this archer, the draw length is perfect. The nock is directly below the eye, and the string is touching his nose, giving him an additional reference point.

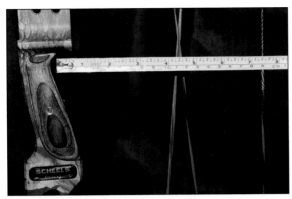

Brace height is measured from the throat of the grip to the string. This bow has a 7³/8" brace height. Brace height has a bearing on the power stroke of a bow.

has a marked rod as an arrow. You come to full draw, settle into your anchor with a slightly bent elbow, then read your draw length on the marked shaft. Typically, the arrow's nock will be directly below your eye. Whether you use a string loop or clip your release directly to the string will also factor into your draw length, as will release type. Many things must be considered.

There are other ways to measure draw length, such as your wingspan, fingertip to fingertip, divided by 2.5, but there are so many variables that this is not a definitive measurement, only an estimate. Also, your draw length may not be a whole number. It could measure out at 29¹/2 inches, and that's important. Many cam designs will allow you to fine-tune your draw length by a half-inch or so. However, some bows have draw-length-specific cams, so avoid buying one until you know your precise draw length. If you do nothing else at a pro shop, at least get your draw length measured by someone who knows what he is doing. Don't even take your money out of your pocket until you know that measurement, and stick to it religiously.

Brace height? When studying bows, pay attention to the brace height, the distance from the throat of the grip to the bowstring. This is a critical measurement, because it can determine how "forgiving" a bow is. That's a term you'll hear a lot, but "fussy" works, too. Bows with low brace heights, less than seven inches, tend to be louder but faster due to the longer power stroke. However, because the arrow is on the string for a longer period of time during the release, and more susceptible to influence from your grip or bow arm movement, a low brace height is less forgiving.

A higher brace height gives you a shorter power stroke and less arrow speed, as a rule, but it's also more tolerant of minor mistakes in form or release. There are exceptions with some bow and cam designs. A bow with a long, straight riser and short parallel limbs may have a brace height under seven inches and still be a forgiving bow. It's because that design keeps your hand in line with the limb bolts. If a riser is radically reflexed, a design used to create short brace heights, your bow hand will be well behind the limb bolts, and that magnifies grip torque and other shooting technique errors.

Bottom line, if you have excellent form and a crisp release, you may be able to handle a "speed" bow with a low brace height. If you're like the rest of us and just want consistency in your bowhunting, look for a brace height between seven and eight inches.

Draw weight and letoff? It's also possible to "overbow" yourself with a compound. If you're young and in shape and plan to hunt larger game such as elk or moose, a 70-lb. draw weight may be a good choice. However, if you're just hunting deer, bears, antelope, or turkeys, a 60-lb. draw weight may be better. In fact, a properly set-up 60-lb. bow will fling an arrow only about 10 fps slower than a 70-lb. bow, because it can use lighter arrows. Even 50 lbs. will get the job done on all kinds of game, provided you've correctly matched your arrows (see Chapter 2) and broadheads.

Lighter draw weights will also save wear and tear on your joints, and you'll be able to draw your bow smoothly and easily. That's especially important when a buck is 10 yards away on a cold, calm morning. Keep in mind, most compound bows shoot better, quieter, and more consistently when set at their maximum draw weight. Turning a 70-lb. bow's

Finding the right bow should begin with a trip to an archery pro shop where you can get expert advice and see a large selection of bows.

limbs down to 60 lbs. puts slack in your bowstring and buss cables and is simply not as efficient.

The percent letoff on the cams is another choice to be made. Many bow manufacturers offer 65% letoff as an option, but most bows leave the factory at 75 or 80%. It's a matter of preference. To some, the higher letoff can feel too light at full draw, as though the string needs a push to get going. It also means you have less weight on your release or fingers. For example, a 70-lb. draw with an 80% letoff means you're only holding 14 pounds at full draw. That can make your release more critical.

The same bow with a 65% letoff would require that you hold 24$\frac{1}{2}$ lbs. at full draw. That extra draw weight tends to make your release crisper and less affected by error.

Some states may have regulations specific to the percent of letoff, so be sure to check it out before you choose a bow.

Cost? This is a big factor for some bowhunters, particularly the novice who is looking for his first bow and isn't sure if bowhunting is for him. He doesn't want to invest a lot of dollars on an experiment. Even the most economically priced bows can be shot with deadly accuracy. Successful bowhunting is more a culmination of the effort spent in practice, scouting, and the field.

We all know the value of quality equipment. The saying, "You get what you pay for," is true as long as it's within reason. You'll find if you shoot and compare a low end bow to a top-of-the-line flagship bow, the differences in smoothness of draw, arrow speed, hand shock, and overall workmanship will be noticeable. How much the relationship between quality and cost affects your decision is a personal thing.

For a first bow you'd be well served to, once again, stay away from the extremes. You can buy a very good bow in the $400 range. Add accessories such as a sight, arrow rest, and quiver, and you're in business. Or consider a "package" bow already fitted with accessories. Many bow companies are matching up rests, sights, and quivers to their bows in an effort to make your decisions easier. If you're certain you'll love bowhunting, or you have experience and want to upgrade, you can easily drop $1,000 on an upper level bow with high-performance accessories.

QUICK TIPS

- It may be a good idea to visit more than one pro shop so you get a good cross-section of bow models to look at. If they'll let you, shoot several bows. The differences will be noticeable, and when you find your bow, you'll know it.

- When shopping for bows, keep in mind that IBO speed ratings are generally optimistic and derived by shooting a 350-grain arrow from a 70-lb. bow with a 30-inch draw. Manufacturers tend to fudge a bit, so if you aren't getting that kind of speed, don't be concerned. Few do.

- When examining bows, take special note of the grip. How does it feel to you? Some prefer thin narrow grips, others wider, fuller designs. Only you know what feels good to you.

- My advice is to avoid hand-me-down bows. Uncle Bob's bow up in the attic is probably the wrong draw length, and the string and cables have probably crept enough to throw the bow out of sync. You can get a used bow that fits by visiting an archery pro shop.

- Join your local archery club. By hanging around with experienced bowhunters you'll quickly learn what bows are selling well. Archers are never at a loss for words when it comes to recommending equipment.

- Ask what kind of strings are on the bows you're looking at. Serious archers often replace factory strings with custom-made strings from companies like Winner's Choice, Stone Mountain, or Vapor Trail. Some bow manufacturers include high-quality strings and buss cables right from the factory. Others make their own strings. Some are good, some are not and will creep and/or stretch. This can be important, as you'll read in following chapters.

Some bow designs require split limbs, but functionally there is little difference between solid and split limbs.

- Bow manufacturers are including limb dampeners, string suppressors, and other silencing products on their bows from the factory. Take note of what comes with a particular bow, and read more on silencing your bow in Chapter 7.

- If you plan to hand your bow down to a younger bowhunter, you might look for a bow with adjustable draw length, usually done by changing modules on the cams. Better yet, fit a kid with a youth bow built specifically to grow with the youngster. Most bow companies have put a lot of effort into their youth bow line. Look them over closely.

- Consider the mass weight of the bows you're looking at. If your hunting style involves lots of hiking in high country, a lighter bow in the four-pound range (with no accessories) is nice. If you're a treestand hunter, you might prefer a heavier bow that absorbs shock and is easy to hold steady. That said, there's only about two pounds difference between the lightest and the heaviest hunting bows, so don't focus too much on mass weight.

- I don't like bows with all sorts of shiny parts like silvery cams and reflective limb surfaces. Some can act like signal mirrors. I'm looking for a killing machine, not a fashion statement. A nice dull camouflage job is all you need.

- There is little to no difference between bows with solid or split limbs. It's a personal preference having more to do with aesthetics than function.

Buying a bow can be a nerve-racking experience. You'll get more advice than you can use. Consider the points above, get some direction from experienced archers and a reputable pro shop, then play around with the bows you're considering. Most pro shops will let you shoot several models so you can get a feel for the widely varied designs. Be objective and listen to your conscience. One of those bows will talk to you. It'll call your name and your decision will be made.

Obviously, I have not ventured deeply into the highly technical world of bow design. I haven't covered energy storage and transfer, bow efficiency, various force-draw curves, specific cam designs, hysteresis and other complex topics because those topics are for another book and another author. I'm just a bowhunter and don't need to know all the science. I tend to worry more about where a muley buck is going to bed down, if I can get a bull elk to come to my bugling, or whether I should use a whitetail buck or a doe decoy, or both.

Those are the kinds of complex problems I like to solve.

CHAPTER TWO

Correct and consistent spine is the most important quality in the "right" arrow. Static spine is measured by suspending a 1.94 lb. weight from the center of a shaft and the deflection is stated in thousandths of an inch. Arrow selection charts are easier but not foolproof.

The Right Arrow

They called it The Horse Killer. Why? Because there were 27 switchbacks in the steep, nasty trail leading out of British Columbia's Kootenay Mountains. Hunting buddy, Kendall Bauer, and I were on horseback, bows slung over our shoulders – just in case. We'd just started riding down The Horse Killer when it happened, right in front of me.

Kendall's horse slipped off the trail, slammed head first into a tree and rolled down the mountain. Kendall frantically bailed off on the uphill side, avoiding serious injury. After just one complete roll, the horse caught itself and stood up against a tree.

Kendall checked for broken or twisted body parts and then began to assess the damage to his bow. The sight guard was bent over, and of the five carbon arrows in his quiver, the center shaft was snapped in two!

If you've ever tried to break a carbon arrow, you understand how freaky it was that only the center arrow was broken, the rest unscathed.

The point? Even carbon arrows are not immune to damage in the field. Now, some might say if he'd been using aluminum arrows, all five would have been bent. Maybe, maybe not. In any case, the durability of your shafts should rank behind other factors when choosing the right arrow.

What's number one? Correct and consistent spine. Spine, or the stiffness of the arrow shaft, is crucial to a well-tuned bow. Static spine is measured with a spine tester by suspending a 29-inch shaft on two points 28 inches apart. A 1.94-lb. weight is hung from the center of the shaft and the amount of deflection, in thousandths of an inch, is measured. This determines the spine relative to arrow selection charts.

Dynamic spine is the flex in the arrow as it leaves the bow. The draw weight, length of the arrow, and the weight of the broadhead all have a huge bearing on dynamic spine. A longer arrow is more limber, a shorter one stiffer. A heavier broadhead effectively makes your arrow shaft more limber (decreased dynamic spine) because of added resistance to thrust. The opposite is true for lighter broadheads.

As bowhunters, we're especially concerned with dynamic spine because it varies so much from hunter to hunter, arrow to arrow, bow to bow. An ultra-high-speed bow with a very aggressive cam may require a stiffer arrow than an arrow selection chart might indicate.

Complicating this issue is the fact that each manufacturer uses a different labeling system on their shafts, so the numbers you see are only relevant to their particular shafts. Some use actual spine deflection measurement, others use draw weight range, but none are the final word on your personal spine requirements.

Some experimentation is necessary here. Arrow selection charts are merely guides to get you in the ball park. You'll still have to shoot various arrow shafts to see which best fits your equipment, body, and shooting style.

For example, while setting up a PSE X-Force in 2007, the arrow chart indicated I needed a Carbon Force arrow shaft in size 300. However, Pete Shepley, PSE founder, told me not to be surprised if a 200 would fly well. I struggled to tune the

Arrow weight is also crucial to consistent accuracy. A simple scale measures arrow weight in grains. The average hunting arrow, without tip, weighs 250 to 350 grains. This fletched arrow weighs 312.5 grains. Add a 100-grain broadhead and it's lethal.

300s, so I tried the lighter spined shaft and it flew beautifully. I never argue with success.

Whenever I'm tuning a bow, pulling my hair out and trying everything I can think of to get arrows to fly, incorrect spine usually ends up being the culprit. You don't have to purchase new arrows to find the problem. Simply increase or decrease your bow's draw weight and note how it affects arrow flight. If a heavier draw helps, your arrows are over-spined. If lowering your draw weight helps, you need stiffer arrows.

Next on your arrow agenda would be consistent arrow weight. Whether you use a light or a heavy shaft, weight variation from shaft to shaft must be minute. That's because we're dealing with a relatively slow projectile (from 200 to 300 feet per second) and trajectory is greatly affected by the weight of the arrow. If your arrows vary, so will your point of impact.

Straightness is an important quality but much less a factor than spine and weight. Yes, you can take your archery to the highest technical degree, measuring and sorting your shafts according to spine, weight, and straightness. If that's what gives you pleasure, knock yourself out. But for hunting ranges, averaging 15 to 40 yards, arrow straightness is overrated, especially when you're talking about one to three thousandths of an inch difference. Get the straightest arrows you can afford, but just remember spine comes first.

Here are a couple of truths when choosing between quality arrow shafts. Aluminum arrows tend to be straighter and are definitely more consistent in spine and weight. Carbon arrows have a higher stiffness-to-weight ratio and the range of spine is wider. In other words, one size of carbon arrow will cover a wider range of bowhunters' draw weights, arrow lengths, and tip weights. That tends to make your options narrower for carbon arrows, simplifying the discovery of the arrow with the right spine for you.

In most situations, carbon arrows are more durable. They do bend, but not under practical situations, and spine can deteriorate after many, many shots; but again, not so as the average bowhunter would notice. If you happen to drop your bow, or get run over by a moose, chances are your carbon arrows will come out of it either snapped off or straight. Aluminum arrows may not survive such abuse.

It's mostly a personal preference, but the majority of today's bowhunters choose carbon shafts. Quality carbon shafts are produced by Carbon Express, Easton Technical Products, Beman, Gold Tip, PSE Carbon Force, Trophy Ridge, and others. Easton Technical Products rules the aluminum arrow market. Shafts that combine carbon and aluminum, with carbon as either the inside or outside layer, are typically top-quality arrow shafts with a blend of qualities. Examples are Easton's ACC shafts or their Full Metal Jackets.

Now to the arrow weight argument. A constant debate revolves around which penetrates best — a fast, light arrow or a heavy, slow arrow?

Kinetic energy is most often used to determine the potential penetration capability of a particular bow setup.

The formula for kinetic energy is: Mass x Velocity x Velocity/450,240. Mass is arrow weight in grains and velocity is arrow speed in feet per second. Divide that result by 450,240 and you end up with kinetic energy in ft. lbs.

Arrow options are mind-boggling but fall into three categories—aluminum, carbon, and a combination of the two materials. Carbon arrows dominate the market.

You'll need to weigh your arrow/tip combination and shoot it through a chronograph to obtain the factors for that formula. Again, it's not a definitive indicator of penetration, but it does give you some ability to conduct comparative analysis. If you plan to hunt only deer, black bears, and antelope, 35 to 50 foot pounds will do the trick. Elk, caribou, hogs, and other tougher game might require up to 65 foot pounds, and if you plan to hunt extra large or dangerous game like moose or cape buffalo, you'll want to generate somewhere around 70 to 80 foot pounds or more.

As I mentioned, that's simply a standard to guide you. Certainly, large, dangerous animals have been taken successfully with light tackle, but it usually doesn't pay to tempt fate with lesser gear.

The right combination of arrow speed and weight can zip through the largest big game. A 463-grain arrow/broadhead combination easily passed through this big-bodied New Mexico bull elk.

Momentum, others believe, is a better indicator of how well an arrow will penetrate. As a matter of simple physics, a slower, heavier object will not slow down as quickly upon impact as a faster, lighter object. Talk to any highly experienced bowhunter planning to hunt large, dangerous game, and he'll likely be using heavy arrows, maybe even with weight tubes inserted in the shaft, and large, heavy broadheads. That should give you an indication of the benefits of a heavy arrow.

The formula for momentum is: Arrow Weight in grains (mass) x Velocity in feet per second, divided by 225,400. The final result is expressed in slug-ft/secs. How that relates to penetration of live animals is anybody's guess, but that should be enough mathematics to give you a headache. It does me.

I'm in the camp that believes a heavier arrow penetrates best. I also like fast arrows. Even more than that, I like two holes in the animals I shoot. Consequently, I prefer arrow/broadhead combos that weigh from 400 to 475 grains and arrow speeds of 260 to 280 fps and up. That puts my kinetic energy anywhere from 65 to 83 ft. lbs., and that's plenty for any game I might be hunting.

This debate is so volatile because it is impossible to replicate shooting a live animal. Comparing various combinations of bows, arrows, and broadheads cannot be done with real-world accuracy. You'll read more about this in Chapter 8, but unless you're shooting very low draw weights (under 50 pounds), penetration won't be an issue on well-placed shots.

My advice is to find something in the middle. A good rule of thumb is an arrow shaft that weighs from 8 to 10 grains per inch. If you prefer a heavier shaft, then something in the 11 to 13 grains-per-inch range would be an excellent choice for elk and moose. If you're planning an antelope or mule deer hunt, a lighter shaft around 6 to 7 grains per inch will flatten your trajectory for those longer shots. Determine which shaft is the right spine for your bow, and as long as it's not at either extreme in weight, you'll do fine.

But we're not done. There's yet another debate to address – vanes or feathers! First, let's look at arrow cresting and wraps. Cresting your arrows can grow into an art but it is also considerable work. Using adhesive wraps is much easier and will add about one-third the weight of a paint job.

The two primary reasons for either are increasing visibility and fletching adhesion.

To some it seems counterproductive to dress up in camo and face paint then carry a quiver full of brightly colored arrows. The goal is to see the flight of the arrow to accurately determine point of impact. It's always important to know exactly where you hit an animal so you know how to proceed in the aftermath. A cap and crest, or a wrap, can enhance the visibility of your arrow, especially in low light.

QUICK TIPS

- When selecting carbon arrows, make sure they're of high enough quality that their spine is consistent. Poor quality carbons will vary greatly in spine and you'll have "flyers."
- One advantage to using aluminum shafts is obvious when practicing on 3-D targets. Some carbon arrows can be difficult to pull out of a 3-D target as they seem to seize up. Easton's Full Metal Jacket shafts combine carbon shaft qualities with an aluminum outer layer that's easier to remove from a target.
- When seeking the correctly spined arrow, make certain those you're testing are the correct length. Even an inch difference in length can alter the spine of a shaft. Some archers cut their shafts a half-inch beyond the arrow rest launcher, while others prefer them a half-inch beyond the riser for safety's sake.
- Should you decide to change your bow's draw weight, ie, lowering poundage during cold weather hunts, your arrow spine may no longer be correct. Adding a heavier tip may compensate for the change, but make certain you practice after any significant adjustments.
- To hunt extra-large, dangerous game, increase total arrow

weight by slipping weight tubes inside your shafts. They come in 2 or 3 grain-per-inch versions. Some bowhunters have even slipped one arrow shaft inside another (aluminum) or filled their arrow with sand to get the weight they wanted. That's probably overkill with the speed of today's bows.

- Lighter arrow/broadhead combinations have a flatter trajectory and allow you a bit more room for error when it comes to yardage estimation. However, the speed of sound is around 1,100 feet per second, so no matter how fast your setup the sound of your bow will get to the animal first.

- My advice is to buy a fletching jig, such as a Bitzenburger, Bohning, JoJann, or Arizona E-Z Fletch Pro Jig. You can easily learn to fletch your own arrows, either for repair or from scratch.

- If you want to build your own arrows, you'll need a high-speed cutoff saw for carbons, but a copper tube cutter like those plumbers use will cut aluminum arrows. Just don't use it for carbon or combination shafts.

- A shaft "squaring" tool, like the one made by G5 Outdoors, is handy for making sure your shaft ends are square before you glue your inserts.

- The color of your fletching is merely personal preference. White is most visible to humans, video cameras, and game animals, though I've never had a problem with game spooking from my fletching. Colors such as orange, red, and pink are highly visible to humans, less so to game animals. Studies have shown deer can distinguish yellows and blues. When videotaping hunts, I use white wraps, two white vanes and chartreuse, pink, or red for a cock vane.

- Avoid using different styles of nocks in your arrows. Varying

If you're concerned about a column of bright arrows in your quiver, a fletch cover over all but one arrow works well. I've used a net facemask tucked under the shaft in the shaft gripper of the quiver to cover my fletching in situations where I thought the brightness might spook game. There are products on the market intended for that purpose, and they work fine.

I've switched to using wraps on all the arrows I build now, mostly because of enhanced glue adhesion. When I glue a vane or feather to a wrap, I know it's going to stay there. If you use a bare aluminum or carbon shaft and don't clean the shaft correctly, or in some cases, clean the vane base, you could have problems with fletching coming loose. On a New Mexico hunt years ago, I leaned a couple of tightness (how they fit your bowstring serving) can make a difference in your point of impact. You can adjust them by dipping in hot water and pinching or spreading the nock apart.

- Lighted nocks, such as Easton's Tracer Nock or Lumenoks, really help you determine your point of impact, but they're illegal in some states, so check your regulations.

- It's a good idea to use a fine marker to number your arrows by writing on the vanes. As you practice, pay attention to flyers. If a specific arrow tends to fly off the mark, it's easier to keep track of if it's numbered.

- If you insist on using feathers in wet weather, treat them with Bohning Archery's Feather-Dri powder, dry fly dressing, or slip tiny plastic bags over each feather, poking the shaft through first, and pulling it off before knocking the arrow.

- Use high-quality adhesives when fletching your arrows or gluing inserts. Bohning Platinum, Tim's Goat Tuff Glue, AAE Fastset Gel (not for feathers) are excellent for fletching, and Carbon Express Expressbond glue is great for inserts. For aluminum arrows you'll need hot melt glue.

- When choosing fletching for arrows tipped with large, heavy broadheads, go with larger fletching and maximum rotation to stabilize the arrow.

- I recommend using arrows with nocks that can be rotated in the shaft (all carbon arrows offer this feature) so you can orient your fletching for optimum arrow rest clearance. Slow-motion video has shown there is virtually no rotation of the arrow before it passes the rest launcher, so keep that in mind when adjusting nock position.

- Always be aware of any state/provincial bowhunting regulations that pertain to arrow weight, broadhead weight, and shaft length.

practice arrows against the tent and after a rain discovered most of my feathers on the ground. They had spontaneously popped off because I'd done something wrong (still don't know what) in the fletching process.

With wraps, those fears are gone, plus I can see my arrows in flight. That's two problems solved with a wrap that adds only 8 to 10 grains of weight to my shafts and even less when I cut them in half, just long enough for the vane to fit.

Once my shafts are wrapped, it's time to fletch them up. Here's where the debate fires up. Maybe a hunting story will illustrate my personal position in the feathers vs. vanes battle.

It was so cold it hurt to inhale. Decembers get like that in North Dakota. I was trying to fill my deer tag before it was time to change calendars, and any deer would do. I'd struggled to get out of bed that morning, and when I saw the thermometer read -5 degrees, I questioned my own sanity. I do that a lot.

The snow was "squeaky" cold, making it easy to hear the deer coming through the draw. I figured it was a doe, but instead a nice 5x5 buck sneaked toward me, heading for his bed. It was so calm and quiet the sound of his hooves in the frozen ground was deafening.

I prepared for the shot, but the buck didn't present an angle until he was almost under me. As I reached my anchor point, a feather on my arrow rubbed against my bulky knit facemask, making a scratching sound. It might as well have been a firecracker. An explosion of snow and oak leaves was all that remained where the buck had stood.

It's usually not a good idea to set your standards based on a single experience, but I've shot vanes ever since.

Ballistically, feathers are lighter than plastic vanes, but their rough surface creates more drag in flight. A feather may start off a few feet per second quicker, but a plastic vane will catch up eventually. Tests have indicted there's a point downrange, 30 to 40 yards, where vanes overtake feathers, but for practical hunting purposes, in real hunting situations, the speed difference between the two is irrelevant.

The drag that feathers create will stabilize your arrow quicker, and because a feather is much more forgiving of rest contact, they are a good choice for static rests that don't drop away and for finger shooters using static rests.

Vanes are more durable and virtually weatherproof. When conditions are wet, feathers won't hold up well. You can treat them with powders and liquid waterproofing agents, but in my experience, that waterproofing dissipates with contact such as rubbing against brush or clothing. A wet feather will still fly, but the water they hold will affect your accuracy. I prefer the carefree life of using vanes and often use the shorter, high profile vanes that are stiffer and lighter than four or five-inch vanes.

You'll have to decide whether to use right or left helical, offset, or straight fletching configurations on your arrows. Because we're looking at everything from a bowhunter's view, I'd suggest you avoid straight fletch. Broadheads are like tiny wings, and stable flight requires some rotation. The bigger the broadhead, the more rotation is needed.

Offset is essentially a straight fletch with the front and back ends of the vane or feather offset several degrees. I prefer the increased rotation of a helical orientation, where the fletching sort of curves around the shaft. There's no difference between right or left helical as far as arrow flight, but a right helical will spin your arrows clockwise, which will keep your field points and broadheads tight. If you use feathers, which are only fletched in a helical manner, make certain to match your fletching jig clamp, ie., right-wing feathers in a right-wing clamp or vice versa.

Yet another decision is the size and shape of your fletching. Feather users generally go with either four-inch or five-inch feathers and either parabolic or shield cut, which is an aesthetic option for the most part. You'll have a lot more choices in vanes. Bowhunters are having success with three, four and five-inch vanes in

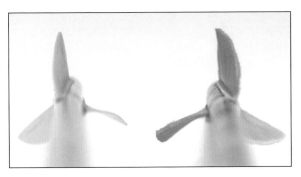

Examples of fletching orientation. (above)The left is a plastic vane fletched right-wing helical, the right a feather fletched left-wing helical. (left) The left is a Blazer vane fletched straight and right is a plastic vane fletched offset.

the traditional parabolic shape, but the newer, shorter, higher-profile vanes, such as the two-inch Bohning Blazers have taken a huge chunk of the market. New Archery Products offers a similar-shaped vane, the QuikSpin, which features a "kicker" fin that maximizes rotation. Both come in various lengths.

A unique option is something called a FOB, which stands for Fletching Only Better. This "ring wing" device, manufactured by Starrflight, is an alternative to fletching that slips over the back of your arrow shaft. It's designed to impart rotation to your arrow then pop off upon impact. They're easy to install, fly well even in the wind, and will actually mark the spot where your animal was hit.

Before closing, I should mention arrow balance, otherwise known as Front of Center, or FOC. To fly well, your arrow needs a certain amount of balance, with the tip being slightly heavier than the tail. For most of us bowhunters, FOC is a non-factor because standard arrow/broadhead configurations are balanced. If you go to extremes in the size of your fletching or the weight of your arrow shaft and broadhead, you might run into balance problems.

To determine the FOC of your arrow, balance a completed arrow with fletching and broadhead on a fulcrum of some type and mark the arrow at the balance point. Measure total arrow length and mark the linear center. Divide the distance between your two marks by the complete arrow length and multiply by 100. Anywhere from 9 to 13 percent is fine, and you should no longer concern yourself with FOC. Just go hunting.

Custom-building your own arrows adds enjoyment to your bowhunting. Here are examples of fletching jigs (from Bohning and Bitzenburger), arrow shafts, plastic vanes, feathers, arrow wraps, and glue. Note the FOBs on the left.

Some bowhunters love the gadgetry and challenge of fine-tuning their bowhunting gear. Spending the time and effort to custom-build arrows to their personal specifications, fits that personality. I do it because I have certain requirements and prefer to rely on myself.

If you feel the same way, the only thing left to say is—Have fun!

CHAPTER THREE

These are examples of static "capture" arrow rests. These are proven hunting rests, and the Whisker Biscuit (top) is easily the most popular rest on the market.

Arresting Arrow Rests

If my memory serves me correctly, it was minus four degrees that morning. Strapped high up in a big cottonwood in North Dakota, I was frozen almost as stiff as Jeremiah Johnson's buddy, Hatchet Jack.

The morning had been quiet, so I climbed down and trudged through a frozen wetland, dotted with Russian olive trees, toward my truck. I hadn't gone far when I spotted a buck running toward me, sun glinting off sweeping pearl-white antlers. I dropped to my knees while quickly loading an arrow.

The buck was either chasing or being chased, but I didn't care; I just wanted him to stop. When he was about 30 yards away (there were no laser rangefinders back then) I bleated with my mouth and the buck stopped broadside and burned a hole in me with his eyes.

Struggling against heavy clothing, cold muscles, and a 70-lb. draw weight, I managed to get my bow back only to have my arrow hop off the dual-pronged arrow rest!

Reaching up with my left index finger, I frantically tried to get the arrow where it belonged, but the cold and my heavy wool gloves had stolen my dexterity. Helplessly, I watched the buck stare at me for a few seconds, puzzled by my one-finger contortions, then bound off into the snow-filled cattails.

The silence of that calm, cold morning was broken only by my soft uncontrollable whimpering.

I can't remember exactly what brand of arrow rest was on that bow, but I do know one thing — it was a shoot-through prong rest. That type of arrow rest has lost its popularity among bowhunters in recent years and for good reason. Had I been using one of the popular arrow rests of today, that buck likely would have died that cold morning. My logic will become apparent as you read further.

I recommend two types of arrow rests for the modern bowhunter, a static "capture" rest or a "drop-away" rest.

By capture rest, I'm referring to the various arrow rests that "arrest" your arrow shaft from the moment you load it onto the string until the launch cycle is complete. Having complete control of your arrow is often crucial in those tense, unpredictable moments like the one described above.

One of the most popular hunting rests to come along in years is the Whisker Biscuit. It's simple, installs easily, captures your arrow, and it works. For most hunting situations this is a very good choice. Young archers will also like this style of rest because it eliminates the common problem of the arrow coming off the rest as kids struggle to reach and maintain full draw.

Other versions of the same concept include BowTech's Hostage arrow rest and the NAP Quiktune 360 CaptureRest, both of which are static rests that capture your arrow.

If this type of rest has a negative side, it's that it can be a bit noisy when an arrow is drawn across it on a cold, calm day. Some arrow shaft surfaces are noisier than others, so you'll have to experiment. Trophy Ridge arrows feature a slick, "Silent Slide" coating that makes them quiet in this type of arrow rest. Silicon spray on the rest can reduce noise and also repels moisture, which can be a problem, especially if it freezes.

The Whisker Biscuit can cause wear and tear on fletching over time because of the constant contact. Feathers slip through more easily but will eventually fray. A tougher vane, such as a Bohning Blazer, will hold up better than a softer, thinner plastic vane. The other two rests I mentioned have gaps in the bristles to accommodate the path of your fletching, so there is less wear.

I wish I'd invented the Whisker Biscuit (I'd be able to afford my own land), but for my bowhunting I prefer a drop-away arrow rest for several reasons.

First, if installed correctly, there's zero fletching contact, which means no

These are examples of drop-away arrow rests with some degree of arrow containment.

impact on arrow flight. You can make your adjustments as you tune your bow with no concern about the fletching glancing off the rest launcher. This makes setting up a drop-away rest quick and easy, because you're not dealing with two problems at once.

One thing you'll notice in the following pages as we look at all sorts of equipment, is that I'm a fanatic when it comes to silence. I don't tolerate unnecessary noises of any kind at any time. Period. Maybe that's a bit picky, but it's reality for me.

Consequently, the silence of a drop-away rest has captured my heart. I can apply one of bowhunting's greatest inventions — adhesive fleece — to my arrow launcher and know, without question, my arrow will be deathly quiet as I draw my bow. Silence, at that precise moment in my hunt, is so crucial I simply won't tolerate anything less.

Yet another benefit is the durability of that silence. Because the arrow contacts the rest launcher for only a portion of the draw and launch, my fleece lasts throughout the season. With the static rests of yesteryear, the fleece eventually wore out and it seemed I always needed to install new fleece just about the time my bow was shooting perfectly. I hated that!

Some drop-away rests also offer the same total arrow containment as a Whisker Biscuit. The Trophy Taker TC, QAD Ultra Rest, and the Ripcord are examples. The Trophy Taker features a containment frame around the launcher, while the other two rests employ a launcher that doubles as a containment device.

Some drop-away rests, such as the one from Schaeffer Performance Archery, have launchers with prongs that capture your arrow in all but the most severe angles. In other words, you can't turn your bow past horizontal, but that's seldom a problem.

Other styles of drop-away rests don't offer containment per se, but you can simply install a small adhesive arrow clip on the riser shelf that will hold your arrow shaft until the launcher picks it up as you draw.

Whether I'm in a treestand hunting whitetails or on my belly preparing to draw on a bedded muley buck, I appreciate knowing my arrow will be where I need it, when I need it, and do so quietly. Cold weather or not. Torque or not. Big buck or not.

A word of caution. Just because

For arrow rests that don't include an arrow containment feature, an adhesive arrow holding clip can be installed on the riser shelf. These devices will hold your arrow quite securely.

your arrow rest captures your arrow doesn't mean you should be walking around with a loaded arrow. That's never a good idea. All it takes is a stumble and you could end up finding out just how lethal your broadheads can be. I can't imagine lying there, thinking of my family, and waiting to bleed to death!

When hunting on the move, never load an arrow until just prior to the shot.

Some drop-away rests eliminate the need for a specific "cock" feather orientation, while others may require a cock feather or vane to be up or down. In an emergency, it may not make a huge difference, but that's also the case with a Whisker Biscuit. That's a huge improvement over yesterday's static rests.

Install a Whisker Biscuit like you would any rest. Set the arrow height so the level shaft bisects the rest mounting hole. This may vary on some bows. Hoyt suggests the bottom of the arrow shaft bisect the center of the rest mounting hole on some of their bows. Also, be sure the Biscuit is perpendicular to the arrow shaft.

For centershot, start by holding the bow at arm's length and look down on the bowstring, lining it up with the valley of the lower cam. With an arrow in the Biscuit, position the rest so the arrow shaft is directly in line with the travel of the bowstring. You may also be able to press an arrow shaft against the riser shelf and line up your loaded arrow so it is parallel with the shaft you're using for alignment. Keep in mind, this will only get you close. Minor adjustments will likely be necessary to achieve good arrow flight.

Follow that same initial procedure with a drop-away. You may have to prop up

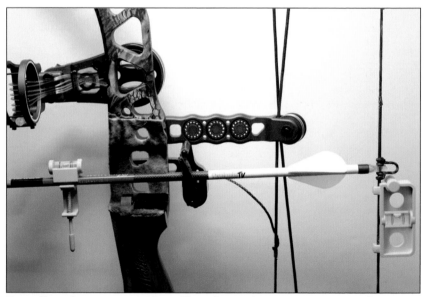

Regardless of arrow rest used, you'll need to set it up as you tune your bow. A set of bubble levels, one for the string and one for the arrow, is very helpful. I've found the best luck with the arrow just a hair above level (perpendicular to the string) at the nock end.

the launcher so you can set the height and centershot. I've had good luck setting my rests so the nock end of my arrows is just slightly above perpendicular to the bowstring. I use a string level with the bow in a bow vise, then an arrow level on the shaft.

Once the rest is in position, you'll need to attach your actuator cord to the down-traveling buss cable so it can pull the rest up as you come to full draw. This can be done with either a small "football" clamp that uses tiny screws, or you can tie it in. A cow hitch with some serving above it to prevent slippage will work too. I prefer to slip the cord between the strands of the buss cable, melt the end into a knob, and then tie it in with serving thread.

Adjust the length of the cord so that your rest launcher comes to its full up position about one to two inches before full draw. This allows your launcher to stay up long enough to guide your arrow yet get out of the way before the fletching arrives. On some rests that adjustment is made at the rest and on others at the tie-off point.

Another arrow rest I like that's a little different is the Limbdriver from Vapor Trail. On this rest, the actuator cord is attached to the upper limb. The rest launcher is under spring tension to stay down, and when you draw back, slack is given

QUICK TIPS

- Once your arrow rest is in place and tuned for perfect arrow flight, tighten it down then take a marker of some type and mark both the vertical and horizontal position on the rest. A quick look will assure you the rest is where it's supposed to be.

- If you do a lot of spot-and-stalk hunting, where you're belly-crawling and laying your bow out in front of you, choose a rest that is built to handle the abuse of landing in rocks, mud, and brush. A rest with a fragile or obtrusive launcher may cause you problems when the going gets tough.

- Arrow speed can be affected by your choice of arrow rest. A Whisker Biscuit may cost you 3 or 4 feet per second, and the lack of friction on a drop-away rest will generally add several feet per second to your arrow when compared to static rests.

- Finger shooters need an arrow rest that provides some side pressure to compensate for the horizontal oscillation of the arrow at release. Spring-loaded plunger rests, or rests with stainless steel launchers below and on the riser-side of the arrow shaft, work well.

- To quiet a drop-away rest at the shot, place a small piece of rubber or several layers of adhesive fleece on the riser shelf where the rest launcher makes contact.

- If you decide to do your own tuning, a laser centershot device is useful. There are at least two models, the EZE-Center from Easy-Eye Archery and the Bowplane from Doubletake Archery. Both use a red laser light to assist you in finding centershot.
- If you're using an arrow-holding clip on the rest and the arrow seems to hop out of the clip as the launcher rises, use a razor blade or small emery board to trim the inside edges of the holder so the shaft comes out easier.
- Be sure to put adhesive fleece on your rest launcher before you tune your bow. It can affect arrow flight if you add it later.
- Once your bow is tuned, load an arrow, then move it all around on the rest, up against the riser, and even up to the bottom of the sight-pin guard. Wherever the shaft contacts metal, cover it with fleece. Even the slightest *clink* can ruin your day or season.

to the cord and the rest comes up. It's very easy to adjust, because you simply pull the cord up snug and tighten the hex screw and it's set. One advantage of this rest is if the actuator cord somehow fails (highly unlikely with any drop-away rest) the launcher pops up and you can still shoot quite accurately because the launcher is spring-loaded. I know; I tried it myself.

The Muzzy Zero Effect arrow rest is another popular option, and it operates off a mechanical arm that attaches to the cable guard or the buss cable on bows with roller guards. As with all equipment mentioned in this book, there will be constant change and innovation. I only mention specific products to give you an idea of the concepts involved. Keep your eyes open for the latest, greatest arrow rest.

Your arrow rest is your primary implement for tuning your bow. This can be a very complex subject, and entire books have been written about the process. Some like to "paper tune" their bows, a method that involves shooting arrows through suspended paper at close range. The goal is to tune the bow for perfect bullet holes. In my opinion, this outdated procedure will give you more headaches than satisfaction. I never shoot through paper anymore, because there are better methods such as walk-back tuning and better yet, broadhead tuning. Here's a brief description of each procedure.

Walk-back tuning — With your bow and correctly spined arrow shooting close to where you're aiming, set up a target with a bull's-eye near the top. Walk back to 20 yards and shoot an arrow at the bull's-eye aiming with your 20-yard pin. Now, walk back to 30 yards and shoot another arrow at the same spot, still aiming with your 20-yard pin. Your arrow will fly low. Walk back to 40 yards and again shoot at the same spot with your 20-yard pin.

You should have a descending line of three arrows. If that line of arrows angles to the left, move your arrow rest to the right in very small increments, one-sixteenth inch or so. If your arrows angle to the right, move your rest to the left. Continue this process until your arrows are vertically aligned. When that happens, the arrow rest is at your all-important centershot. Some fine tuning of your rest height may be necessary, but I usually start off with my arrow perfectly perpendicular to the bowstring, or just slightly high at the nock end, and seldom make another adjustment. For finger shooters, a higher nocking point may be necessary.

Broadhead tuning — An arrow shot from a poorly tuned bow is infected with flight anomalies. It's not flying straight. When shooting field points this isn't always visible to the archer. Attaching a fixed-blade broadhead to the front of your arrow amplifies those anomalies, making them much more noticeable, which is good. You can't fix what you can't see.

Regardless of the type of broadhead you plan to shoot for hunting, round up six arrows and attach a fixed-blade broadhead (of the same weight as your chosen broadheads) to three arrows and field points (again, same weight) to the other three. Set up a target at 20 yards and shoot your three field points, taking care to shoot as tight, a group as possible. Now, shoot your three broadheads. If your groups are tight you may want to shoot just one broadhead so as not to damage others. Just be sure you're shot is good.

Compare the two groups. If your broadheads are shooting higher than your field points, lower your arrow rest (or raise nocking point). If they are below your field points, raise your arrow rest. If your broadheads are shooting left of your field points, move your arrow rest to the right. If they're to the right, move your arrow rest left. Be sure you always make very small adjustments, maybe as little as one-thirty-secondth inch. The point is, chase your field points by moving your arrow rest toward the field point group. It doesn't matter if you're right or left-handed, the adjustments are the same.

Do not adjust your bowsight at this point unless your arrows are getting close to the edge of your target. We're only worried about arrow flight, not impact point. Keep in mind, both groups will move as you make adjustments and shoot again. However, the broadhead group will move more than the field-point group. Eventually, they will merge into one group. Only then do you adjust your bowsight to bring your group to the bull's-eye.

In my opinion, broadhead tuning is the final word in tuning your bow. It's applicable even if all you do is shoot field points or low-profile mechanicals. If fixed-blade broadheads are flying perfectly, your bow is tuned!

In summary, choose an arresting arrow rest that features adjustability for tuning, durability while hunting, and total silence while drawing and shooting.

If your arrow rest does all that, there'll be less chance you'll find yourself whimpering in the woods. 🦌

CHAPTER FOUR

Hunting without a bowsight isn't easy. Years ago, I took this pronghorn with a recurve, cedar arrows, and no bowsight. Still, I wanted sight pins and went back to modern archery. Too bad I didn't have modern camouflage back then!

Sighting Systems

For three years I abandoned technology and hunted with a Black Widow recurve bow. I shot with a finger tab and used Zwickey-tipped cedar arrows, and the only sighting device I relied on was my brain. It was fun. Unfortunately, I wasn't very good at it.

The first animal I ever drew my recurve on was a bull elk. It was a 14-yard shot, and my arrow easily sliced through his vitals. I also took a nice muley buck, two whitetail bucks, and an antelope buck during those three years.

However, over that period of time I passed on shots at record-class mule deer, antelope, and caribou bulls, because they were just out of my comfortable range of 20 to 25 yards. There were practice sessions when my confidence was solid, but in the presence of game I wasn't so sure of myself. One evening I found myself sitting in a whitetail stand hoping nothing too big came by!

That was my sign. I converted back to modern equipment and haven't looked back.

The primary drawback, at least for me, was the lack of a bowsight. Instinctive shooting can be deadly, but it limited my effective range more than I was willing to accept. I've killed lots of game at less than 10 yards but every now and then I need to take a longer shot. I couldn't come to grips with spending so much time, effort, and money on hunting trips and getting really close but not quite close enough.

A bowsight will make you a more accurate archer – period. Sight pins are indispensable when it comes to maintaining the necessary elevation and windage in your shots. That is, in a nutshell, the purpose of a bowsight.

Another thing a bowsight can do is help you monitor shooting form.

That was evident on a deer hunt in Kentucky in 2006. It was the last day of the hunt, and a good buck came slipping through the thick brush just before sundown. He came from an unexpected direction, and there was no shooting lane.

I drew my bow and started squatting down, searching for a hole to thread an arrow through. My butt hit the seat of the treestand, but I still wasn't low enough, so I slid off and kept crouching until my lower limb was actually below the level of my treestand platform.

I finally got my sight pin under a horizontal limb but was in such an awkward position I was concerned whether my odd form would affect the shot. Then I noticed I was able to center the round pin guard on my sight, in the center of my peep sight hole. That's when I knew all was right, and I touched it off. The arrow zipped under the limb and hit exactly where I was aiming, killing the nice 4x4.

That shot would not have been possible without a bowsight.

I remember the days when my sight pins were brass and I painted them with pink or white paint for better visibility. Fiber optics have taken over the bowsight market, because they collect ambient light and concentrate it at the tip of the fiber, making it very bright and easily visible in low-light conditions.

Some sight makers are enhancing pin brightness by wrapping the fibers in coils for better light gathering, or even winding the fibers around reflective tape on the sight guard. The tape holds light, or can be charged with a flashlight, and keeps the fibers lit right up to the end of legal shooting light.

Other methods of enhancing the brightness of fiber-optic pins include winding them in a tube underneath a prism that magnifies light. The LimbSaver Prism sight is an example. You can also install a small, battery-powered "blue" light that shines on the fibers, lighting them up. Always be sure to check your local hunting regulations before using any sort of electronic device while bowhunting.

While fiber optics have taken over the sight market, they can be fragile in poorly designed sights. If you're hunting hard on the ground, or you're just rough with your equipment, consider sights that protect the fibers with metal pins or fins. If they look fragile, they probably are.

How many pins do you need? That's a question only you can answer. If you hunt strictly whitetails at very short yardages and restrict yourself to 20-yard shots, a single-pin sight may be all you need. Simple is always good.

A moveable single-pin sight, which allows you to adjust your one pin to preset yardages, is another option. I used a Vital Gear Star Track sight in South Africa and Namibia and enjoyed being able to concentrate on a single pin. From a ground blind, yardages to waterholes were finite, and there was both time and concealment to make necessary adjustments.

The negative of such a sight is having to constantly monitor what yardage it's set for and having to remember to re-adjust before and after a shot. Before the season, it's important to become very familiar with this type of sight, which is also available in multi-pin versions.

The vast majority of bowhunters, including myself, use bowsights with from three to seven pins. Some archers set the top pin for 10 yards, others 20 and those with flat arrow trajectories maybe even 25 yards. Again, familiarity is your friend. If you've been shooting a 10-yard pin for years, you'll probably want to stick with that. If you change,

Fiber optics have revolutionized the bowsight industry. Nearly every sight made is armed with light-gathering fibers to increase visibility in low-light conditions. Note the reflective tape on the round sight guard. Center the guard in the circular vision of your peep sight to help maintain good shooting form.

I used a moveable single-pin sight to take this fine kudu in South Africa. Having one pin to concentrate on in the hide was nice!

especially just before a hunt, your conditioned mind may, in a heated moment, use the wrong pin.

My sights typically have five sight pins set for 20, 30, 40, 50 and 60 yards. If I'm going after pronghorns or mule deer with an ultra-fast bow, I may use a seven-pin sight. Not because I plan to shoot an antelope at 80 yards, but because I may be called upon to take a second finishing shot at such yardages. Hey, I make mistakes too.

For example, in 2007 I was sitting in a Double Bull ground blind in Montana's Powder River bottom when a monster Boone and Crockett-class pronghorn chased a doe past my blind. They didn't stop, and when they slipped off the alfalfa field into some tall grass, I bailed out of the blind and ran across the alfalfa field with my head down.

To make a long story short, I managed to slip to within 50 yards of the lovesick buck. I took the shot, but the buck moved before the arrow arrived and I made a bad hit. I stayed with the buck and shot him again at 71 yards.

Now, I didn't have a 70-yard pin on my PSE X-Force that day, but I did have a 60-yarder. Rather than hold high with my 60-yard pin, here's how I got a more accurate sight picture. I held my 60-yard pin on the pronghorn's vitals then looked to see where my 50-yard pin was in relation to the animal. I simply moved my 60-

yard pin up to that position and released. That technique also works if you're two pins off. There is a point of diminishing returns at very long yardages, so you need to limit those kinds of shots to emergencies. Still, it pays to practice ultra-long shots once in awhile.

With most gear, I'm an advocate of simplicity and clean lines. Some sights are bulky, heavy, engineering nightmares better suited to competitive archery. Micro-adjust sights are fine if you're doing a lot of sighting-in of your bow or changing a sight from one bow to another, but they're generally heavier and more expensive. I prefer a simple, framed sight that's lightweight and doesn't "stick out" all over. Sight it in, lock it down, and forget it.

Most bowsights are available in standard and micro-adjust versions like the two on the right. If you do lots of adjusting, you may opt for the latter. Otherwise, a standard sight is fine. Set it and lock it down.

If you're into gadgetry and precision, there are sights with second and third axis adjustments. The second axis adjustment helps you calibrate the bubble level on the sight so your bow can be held perfectly vertical. This can be an issue when hunting in the high country where tilted horizons and long distances factor into your sight picture. The third axis adjustment squares your sight guard and pins perpendicular to your arrow shaft. Again, these are expensive options and typically add weight to a sight. You have to decide if you need such precision.

A bowsight isn't all there is to a "sighting system." For increased accuracy and consistency, some type of rear sight reference is a good idea. Having two points of reference is especially important when aiming at extreme angles, such as downward from treestands or mountaintops, because it forces you to bend at the waist and maintain proper "T" form, the shape formed by your upper body and arms as you shoot.

QUICK TIPS

- A sight with a removable dovetail mounting system may be useful if you have to pack your bow into a tight spot like a bow case. I've never seen the need, and I typically use a sight with a compact, simple yet strong frame.

- Bowsights with round pin guards are best, because you can center the guard inside the circular field of vision created by your peep. Then use the appropriate pin for the shot. Some prefer to center the pin they are aiming with in the peep hole.

- Aligning the sight guard in a peep hole also allows you to detect bow hand torque and other form errors. Torquing the bow grip will misalign the sight guard and peep hole. It becomes the sort of "subliminal" reference that helped me kill that Kentucky buck.

- When hunting in a pop-up ground blind, your fiber-optic pins won't have light to gather and may look dark. Some hunters use the tiny "blue" lights to light up the fibers in a blind. Another option is a tritium sight pin that glows in the dark for up to 10 years.

- Fiber-optic pins that are too bright on sunny days will "star" in your vision. Place a rubber band over the fiber coils or some other simple cover to block light, then remove it as necessary.

- When traveling long distances to hunt, it may be a good idea to pack an extra sight, especially if you don't have a back-up bow along, as some models can be fragile.

- Pin configuration, whether it's the traditional horizontal design, vertical, or angled, is a personal preference. Functionally, one isn't better than another. It all depends on what looks good to the only eye that matters — yours.

- Bowsights that feature two or three "tracks" for their pins will allow you to set pins close together. If your arrow trajectory is very flat, you'll appreciate that design.

- Most bowhunters learn to "gap" shoot when an animal doesn't have the decency to offer a shot at 10-yard increments. When the shot is 25 yards, for example, some bowhunters imagine a pin between their 20 and 30-yard pins and aim that way. Others simply hold a pin high or low in the vitals. In the latter case, you still need to pay attention to where adjacent pins are situated so you don't hold too high or low.

- If your bow is a real speed burner, you might consider a three-pin configuration with a 25, 45, and 65-yard pin, or some variation of that example. Just make certain you get accustomed to any new sight pin arrangement well before season.

- As you set your sight pins, keep in mind that ultimately, they should all be in perfect vertical alignment. If they are not, either you're changing your grip for longer yardage shots or your bow simply isn't tuned and you need to start from scratch.

- Your sight pins should also be roughly equidistant from each other. In other words, the gap between your 20-yard pin and your 30 should be the same as between the 30 and 40. Depending on your setup, you may find that gap will widen a bit at very long ranges, such as 60 and 70 yards.

- Pendulum sights feature a sight pin that swings into a higher position as you aim downward to compensate for the angle of the shot. However, today's bows and arrows are so fast I don't feel these sights are necessary for the average treestand hunter.

A peep sight installed between the strands of the bowstring is the most common rear sighting reference. Peep sights that employ a rubber cord attached to the buss cable are popular. The rubber cord applies tension to the peep as you draw, compensating for the rotation of the bowstring and aligning it for full vision. The advantages are easy installation and dependable peep alignment. Disadvantages include potential failure of the rubber cord, considerable noise at release, and the loss of a few feet-per-second in arrow speed. I've always feared having the cord break at the buss cable while I'm at full draw and slapping me in

Even in bright daylight the pins of a good fiber-optic sight are very bright. This can be crucial to getting a shot when the sun goes behind the horizon.

the eyeball. That could ruin a hunt!

I prefer a peep sight that doesn't require a rubber cord. A Fletcher Tru-Peep or G5 Meta Peep are two examples of the peep style I use. It does take some effort, and rudimentary knowledge of the use of a bow press, to get such peeps to turn just the right amount, so the peep hole comes into alignment with your eye as you draw.

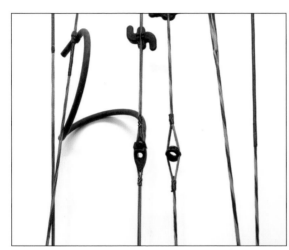

Here are the two primary types of peep sights, one that uses a rubber aligner tube and one that doesn't. Either is deadly as a rear reference point.

A high-quality bow-string that doesn't creep or stretch is a huge help in this regard. A custom bowstring, such as a Winner's Choice, will "settle in" after a couple dozen arrows and then stop creeping. Consistent string rotation, or none at all when you draw, is the goal, so you can always see through your peep.

Should my peep fail to rotate correctly, it usually indicates the string has crept and some adjustment is necessary. I put my bow in a press and add one or two twists to the string to compensate. Not only does that bring my peep back where it belongs, but it restores my bow's axle-to-axle distance to factory specifications.

The advantages of this type of peep are no rubber cord, less loss of arrow speed, because of a lighter load on the string, and no chance of getting smacked in the eyeball. The disadvantages are the hassles of the initial set-up and potential for misalignment when you least expect it. That said, I've never had a peep not turn enough that I couldn't make the shot. By the time my hunt arrives, I know how my peep is performing.

One disadvantage of all types of string peeps is they will cause the iris of your eye to close slightly in response to having that dark object in your vision. This results in loss of light at either end of the day. However, I consider the accuracy and consistency a peep offers to be worth the tradeoff.

Another rear sight option is an alignment device like the Timberline No-Peep or the Anchor Sight. These optical devices are attached to the riser of your bow just out of your line of aiming sight. At full draw you can see a dot or circle in the lens that must be lined up before the shot. Once in alignment, you turn your focus to your sight pins, aim, and take the shot. It takes some practice, but these are pop-

There are many options for a sighting system, but I recommend a no-tube peep like this one to go with a consistent anchor and your nose touching the string. This three-point anchoring technique is very accurate.

ular options for those who want to eliminate a peep from their vision. They also help you maintain good shooting form, because any torquing of the bow prevents alignment.

Then we have bowsights that feature a rear sight like the Hind Sight. A rear aperture contains a crosshair which you line up with a particular sight pin, usually the top one, keeping you and your bow square and lined up. If you need to, use your 30 or 40-yard pin, you would still line up the crosshair on the 20-yard pin to maintain alignment, then place the appropriate pin on the vitals. Again, this type of sight requires plenty of lead time before being used in the field.

QUICK TIPS

- The size of the hole in your peep sight is critical to how well you can see your pins in low-light conditions. Target archers prefer the precision of small peep holes 1/8th inch in diameter or less. For bowhunting, I prefer large holes of 3/8ths to 1/4 inch.

- Another peep sight design sits horizontally in the string with strands separating into two or three slots. As you draw, the peep tilts with the string and provides that rear reference. The Shurz-A-Peep is one example.

- The String-Splitter Peep is essentially half a peep sight that allows better light transmission to your eye. The Myers Predator View peep has an elliptical shape that also works well in low light.

- The Inglewing C-Peep uses a rubber cord, is offset from your bowstring, and features a slot to allow additional light into your eye in mornings and evenings. The Vital Gear Peep Master is a similar concept.

- Some peeps even have small lenses to assist those of us with failing eyesight. They help you see your pins better, but for hunting, I'm leery of this option. In wet or snowy conditions you may not be able to see through your peep at all.

The latest development at this writing is a bowsight that uses electronic LEDs displayed on a tiny screen, similar to the heads-up display used by fighter pilots. The Summit Hot Dot has all sorts of adjustments from choosing the number of dots to a pendulum feature that compensates for downward angles. Since this is an electronic device, be sure to check local hunting regulations before using the Hot Dot.

Bowsight technology has been very active, and it's likely something new and useful will beat this book to press. However, if you keep these options in mind and put in the requisite hours with your chosen sighting system, you'll do fine.

If you choose to shoot your modern compound bow instinctively, without a bowsight, all I can tell you is log lots of practice hours. You're going to need them.

CHAPTER FIVE

If you're concerned about having a column of bright fletching in your bow quiver, get a fletching cover and put it over all but one arrow.

When the stalking gets serious, a bow quiver is essential for keeping a low profile. A hip or back quiver can be very awkward in such intense hunting situations.

Quivering Your Arrows

I just don't get it.

Maybe I'm missing something. Why do some bowhunters refuse to use a bow-mounted quiver for their arrows?

I can understand wanting to be different, or maybe a desire by some traditional archers to keep their bow clean and lightweight, but I fail to see why a modern bowhunter, using a compound bow, would use a hip or back quiver for their arrows.

In Chapter 13, you'll read about a four-hour stalk I made on an Alberta mule deer buck. I spent three and one-half hours of that stalk bellycrawling in grass 15 inches tall. Inching my way across that field with virtually no cover required that I slide my bow ahead then pull myself up to it using my elbows and toes.

Without a bow quiver, where would my arrows have been? Certainly not in a hip quiver, colliding with brush and waving above the grass. A back quiver would have increased my profile and tipped off at least one of the seven bucks bedded in front of me. And sliding my bow ahead of me was tough enough, I sure didn't need a loose quiver to add to that problem. I don't think I could have made that stalk without a bow quiver.

Let's look at each point in this debate:

Not using a bow quiver keeps my bow light and maneuverable. I weighed a popular one-piece bow quiver with five arrows and broadheads, and the total was less than one pound! Some stabilizers weigh that much. I don't feel the weight savings is significant. Besides, in the case of some high-energy bows, the extra weight of a quiver full of arrows will actually contribute to less hand shock and better accuracy.

I don't buy the maneuverability argument either. Many bow quivers ride close to the riser and you'll loose far more mobility if you have a quiver full of arrows strapped to your hip or on your back while walking or crawling through the woods.

I don't like having a column of bright-colored fletching on my bow while aiming and drawing. Yes, a quiver full of brightly fletched arrows does stand out, but I've never had a deer or elk pick me out because it spotted my fletching. It's either my human form or the movement they spot, not the color.

If you want to catch the attention of game, strap a hip quiver to your leg while still-hunting. The waving of your bright fletching will be sufficient to flag down an incoming 747! I've seen some bowhunters use back quivers with fletching sticking out above their heads, or even Cat Quivers with covered fletching compartments, but again, I just don't see it. I do too much ducking under limbs and branches to have something that obtrusive on my back, and fumbling for an arrow in a tense moment isn't cool. Even returning an arrow to a back quiver is a hassle and may require you to take the pack off.

Want more negatives? You can't ride a horse, ATV, or even sit on a hillside without taking a back quiver off. Sorry to be negative, but that's the way I see it.

My bow is more accurate without a bow quiver. This is a myth. If you sight your bow in with the quiver attached and loaded with all but one arrow, you will shoot as accurately, or more so, than with a bare bow. The weight of the quiver has a stabilizing effect, and your accuracy will likely improve. Now, if you're hunting in strong winds on the Great Plains or the Arctic tundra, you may benefit from a removable quiver you can quickly take off so it doesn't catch the wind.

I've done some testing with different bows and various configurations from no arrows in the quiver to full quivers, and I have never seen more than a one-inch difference in my point of impact at 30 yards. In hunting situations, most of us can't shoot well enough to discern a difference in accuracy.

Here are some other negatives of not keeping your arrows on your bow. If you're set up on an incoming elk and you remove your quiver, like I see even some high-profile TV bowhunters do, you're opening yourself to all sorts of problems. Second shots are not common, but they do occur. Getting an arrow out of a loose quiver lying on the ground in front of you causes far more commotion and movement than slipping a second arrow out of bow-mounted quiver. When hunting elk, it's common to have to get up and move as the elk circles downwind. Will you remember to take your quiver with you? What if you miss the first shot and the bull just stands there?

It's not as big an issue in a treestand but still, you'll have to turn around, reach who knows where to grab another arrow, work it out of the quiver, load it, and turn around again. With a bow-mounted quiver you don't even have to take your eyes off the animal. Your arrows are always where you expect them to be.

I also feel your arrows are at greater risk of damage if they're strapped to your back or hip. Should you slip on a wet hillside, fall off a deadfall, or crash your horse or ATV, it's far more likely your arrows, maybe all of them, will be damaged. When they're attached to your bow you'll be less likely to put it, as well as your arrows, at risk.

One final negative involves outfitters. I know many who despise hip quivers, primarily because there will invariably be a time when a client forgets his arrows back in camp. That means an extra trip back to get the arrows when time is usually short.

Now, I could probably come up with more negatives, but that's my opinion on quivers. I know I won't change everyone's mind, and there are plenty of bowhunters who do just fine with hip or back quivers, Chuck Adams to name one (okay, a significant one). But I still don't understand it.

One more point. I often see hunters with only a couple of arrows in their quiver. I never understood that either. A 438-grain arrow weighs exactly one ounce, so shoving two or three more ounces into your quiver shouldn't be a concern. What if you have to follow up a wounded deer and weave another arrow, or two, through brush to finish it? What if you lose an arrow or drop one out of the tree? What if

QUICK TIPS

- If you expect windy conditions but still prefer a bow-mounted quiver, get one that has a quick-detach system so you can remove the quiver before taking the shot. A word of caution. Remember to pick it up if you have to move for a better shot.
- To conceal your bright fletching in a bow quiver, use a fletch cover. PSE makes one that slips over your arrows and elastic loops keep it on. I typically cover all but my "kill" arrow. If necessary, it's very easy to slip a second arrow out of a fletch cover. You can even make your own with a small piece of lightweight, quiet camouflage material.
- Trophy Ridge makes a really nice quiver in both one and two piece models. It has a large rubber band that stretches over the gripper to secure your arrows. That's a great safety feature and will save you from lost arrows, too.
- Line the inside edge of your quiver hood with adhesive fleece to eliminate any clinking noise that may occur when you carefully slip a broadhead-tipped arrow out to make an unexpected shot.
- Be sure to fill your quiver with arrows and take note of any potential contact with parts of your arrow rest and sight apparatus. Some of these products stick out too far and you may need to cover them with fleece. Any noise is a bad noise.
- Some quivers come with hood foam that is very noisy. Rip it out and replace it with something quieter. Ethafoam is too noisy. You need something softer. It also helps if you rub a little cooking oil into the blade and ferrule slots so your broadhead can slip in and out quietly. Don't use Vaseline, as it will collect debris.
- If you don't like the way the foam in your quiver hood fits your chosen broadhead, screw an old broadhead to an aluminum shaft, heat it with a flame, and slide the hot broadhead into the foam. It will melt a custom-made slot for your broadheads.
- Make sure you can insert your broadheads into the quiver foam at various angles. This allows you to turn your shafts so there's no contact with the fletching of adjacent arrows. I like to position the arrows at either end of my gripper, so they can be removed without the fletching coming in contact with the next arrow. I hate noise.

- Because silence is such a big issue with me, quivers are a challenge. They are notorious for generating noise. You won't have to worry about that if you use an Alpine Archery Soft Loc quiver. It's made with a lot of rubber, comes off easily, and is very quiet.

- A quiver hood filled with nothing but air can sound like a drum if a branch slaps it as you slip through the brush. You can quiet it down by covering the hood with adhesive fleece. Attaching a couple of small dampeners from LimbSaver or BowJax can also help.

- Mechanical broadheads may give you problems. When using Rage two-blade heads, I take the quiver foam out and cut off a three-eighths-inch slice and reinstall it in the hood. The tip of the broadhead penetrates just deep enough to stay in place without deploying the blades. This also will work for other types of mechanical heads, but not all.

- Another option for mechanicals is a quiver with two grippers, one near the hood, which now serves only as a cover for the broadhead blades (there is no foam). Kwikee Kwiver and Bohning make such a quiver.

- If you ignore me (maybe wisely) and prefer to hang your quiver up in a tree, you sometimes can get extra brackets that can be screwed into the tree so your quiver is solidly attached. It'll be much easier to get your emergency arrow out of a stationary quiver.

you miss two does then see the buck of a lifetime? If you're carrying only three arrows, and one is a practice arrow (I always carry one in my quiver), you're not leaving yourself much insurance.

Needing more than one, two, or even three arrows is very rare. However, it's better to have five arrows and need only one, than have three and need four. My advice is to carry a full quiver (four to six arrows) at all times. I never carry less than five.

Now that we got the debate out of the way, let's look at some quiver options. The first thing I look for in a quiver of any design is whether it has an adjustable mounting height. By the time I get a broadhead on my arrows they can be 31 inches long, and there are few things I hate more than having my arrow nocks extend beyond my lower cam. In fact, I just won't tolerate it. I often rest my lower cam on my boot, or even on the ground, and I can't afford to have the nocks coming in contact with dirt or rocks. They can fill up with dirt, or even break, but the biggest risk is a cracked nock I don't know about. That can result in both a damaged bow, due to a dry-fire, and a lost animal.

It's only because of angle, but this photo illustrates what you're up against if your arrows extend below your bottom cam. You cannot set the bottom limb of your bow on the ground and risk damage to your nocks. Unknowingly cracking a nock is a worst-case scenario.

With the quiver mounted on my bow, I'll slip a broadhead-tipped arrow into the quiver and see where my nocks are. If they're less than an inch from the bottom edge of my lower cam, I won't use that quiver unless there's a way to adjust the hood upward. Fortunately, many manufacturers have responded to that need.

Some quivers out there are complete junk. There's just no nice way to say it. Bow manufacturers who make quivers to match their bows aren't always the best either. I love the Mathews quivers because they have adjustable grippers, and the quivers from Fuse Accessories are excellent as well. BowTech put some real effort into their quivers, and their new Octane quivers are outstanding — they even feature a magnet in the hood.

If you go with a bow-mounted quiver, you'll have to decide whether you want a two-piece or one-piece removable. A two-piece quiver mounts to the riser, typically on specially designed holes at either end. These quivers are the most stable, strongest, and vibration-free option, and they're low-profile, riding as close to the riser as possible. This is a factor if you're busting your way through alders in Alaska, elk timber in Idaho, or when riding those nasty horses. The thinner the profile, the better.

A one-piece quiver can attach to the standard mounting holes on the riser or bracket specially designed for the quiver, and they usually feature some type of quick-detach device. These quivers tend to be a little noisier, because the single attachment point creates more vibration. Some quick-detach devices also generate noise because they don't lock tight enough. Still, a removable quiver gives you the option to remove it. For me, the only time I remove a quiver is in a ground blind where space is limited and my movements are concealed. If the wind is so strong I can't hold my bow steady with the quiver attached, it's probably too strong to take an ethical shot anyway.

You'll have to choose between a two-piece and a one-piece quiver. A two-piece quiver is more solid and vibration-free and has a lower profile on your bow. A one-piece quiver usually features a quick-detach apparatus, which is very important to some bowhunters.

Though it doesn't necessarily fit the parameters mentioned, the venerable Kwikee Kwiver has long been a favorite of thousands of bowhunters. I may be crazy, but I'm not stupid enough to argue with success. If you have a bow-mounted quiver you like, and it serves you well, that's all that matters.

Since I detest hip and back quivers, I don't have much advice for you. Some models of the Cat Quiver act as your backpack and will hold some of the items you carry daily. I carry far too much gear with me and must use a good-sized daypack.

Hip quivers are great for the 3-D range, but those that strap to your thigh will flash back and forth with every step. Hip quivers attached at the waist will cause less movement, but your arrows are still vulnerable to catching on brush, your pack, and other things as you hunt. Of course, still-hunting, which you could be involved in without warning, is the worst time for hip and back quivers.

I'm not trying to alienate anyone here with my rant about quivers. Many of us get set in our ways, and I'm no exception. However, I can only give you the best advice I know how to give, and that is this: Get accustomed to and use a bow-mounted quiver.

CHAPTER SIX

Hunting buddy Larry D. Jones demonstrates his release form on a Texas hog hunt. He prefers the "one over, two under" approach and uses a tab and a wool glove. This combination feels good to him, so it works.

Releasing the String

I miss my fingers.

When my first bow—a Jennings T-Star—arrived, I was in heaven. The task of building a callous on my right middle finger was enjoyable as I shot arrow after arrow, both indoors and out. My brain was fresh and devoid of bad habits, and I could hold my pin on the bull's-eye as if my arm were encased in concrete. My accuracy and confidence skyrocketed, and when hunting season arrived, I was ready.

A couple of things happened over the next few years. First, I came to the realization that shooting with fingers in ultra-cold weather, a common thing in my home state of North Dakota, was a challenge. What kind of shooting glove or tab could keep my fingers warm? I tried using a hand muff with a light glove and finger tab, and it worked, but my release was never as good as I wanted it to be in cold weather. In short, it was a hassle shooting fingers in cold weather.

Second, I started to develop some bad mental habits. I won't go into the sordid details for fear of planting bad thoughts in fresh minds, but I lost some control of my release, especially when shooting paper bull's-eyes. It's a mental thing, and if you've never had target panic, I advise you to immediately erase this paragraph from your memory.

Mechanical releases came on the scene and were scorned at first, but in an effort to regain some control, I decided to try one. I bought an Allen release that was essentially a hook with a trigger. It took some getting used to, but eventually I became comfortable with it and used it on many hunts for all sorts of game with no problems.

I still miss being able to wrap my fingers around the string as I stalk through the woods, but it's the price I pay for the increased mental control a mechanical release gives me. It also allows me to hunt in all sorts of weather and maintain a crisp, clean release.

You have to make your own decision. Many of today's archers started off with fingers, especially as youngsters, but today the vast majority of bowhunters use mechanical releases. My hunting buddy, Kendall Bauer, is an excellent finger shooter, but he's an endangered species.

If you shoot fingers, you'll have to choose between various types of shooting gloves or finger tabs. Some archers prefer a three-fingered shooting glove, because they can cut three fingers off of a regular glove to accommodate it. A shooting glove stays put and protects your fingers from wear and tear. The down side of a leather glove is string grooves tend to wear into the leather and can impede a clean release. That said, there are some gloves with various types of material inserts or nylon webbing on the fingertips to prevent grooving, and others use a stiffer

Cordovan leather or even slick Cordura fabric. You'll have to experiment to see which you prefer.

Finger tabs tend to provide the finger shooter with a cleaner release. First, you'll have to decide if you want to shoot with two fingers under and one above the arrow, or with three fingers under. It's a personal thing; however, those archers who shoot instinctively tend to like three fingers under, because it puts the arrow closer to their line of eyesight. If you plan to shoot fingers with a sight on your bow, you'll likely need to shoot two-fingers under so you your sights can be positioned further above the arrow's flight path.

Of course, consistency is always the number one consideration in archery, and that's the

A string loop with a trigger-finger release is my favorite method for releasing the string. This is a heavy duty loop. Some prefer thinner diameter loop material.

purpose of a mechanical release. That doesn't mean you can't punch or jerk a mechanical trigger. They are not a cure-all for poor form.

First, decide how you'll attach your release to the bowstring. If you plan to clip your release directly to the bowstring just below the arrow nock, you'll need a release design that won't cause excessive wear on your serving. If it has any sharp edges that will contact the serving, especially at full draw, don't use it. Nothing will put an end to your hunt quicker than a broken string serving.

My recommendation is to use a string loop. Some call it a D-loop but, whatever the name, the advantages of a string loop are many. It almost eliminates wear on your serving, because your release clips to the heavy cord of the loop material. I've never worn out a loop, but I use heavy cord for mine. Some archers prefer a lighter material to save weight, but I like the durability of a heavier cord and the stiffness makes it easier to clip my release on in a tense moment.

A string loop's most important benefit, in my estimation, is that it puts equal draw pressure on both sides of the arrow nock, rather then the considerable upward pressure imparted by a release clipped on the bowstring directly below the nock. This even pressure makes your tuning easier and arrow flight more consistent. And, because the string loop allows you to twist or torque your release without transferring that torque to the bowstring, it is also more forgiving of anchoring inconsistencies.

Consistent use of a string loop also helps keep your peep sight turning correctly, which is especially important if you're not using rubber aligner tubing on your peep.

The only disadvantage of a string loop is if it is not tied correctly it may fail, but in 10 years of using one, I've never had one come untied. The trick is to tie opposing cow hitches and burn knobs on the ends that won't slip out.

You may also opt for an aluminum loop, like the T.R.U.-Nok from T.R.U. Ball, which clamps to your bowstring. They work very well, but you'll need to use the right kind of release for that style so there isn't excessive metal-to-metal wear. You may also discover a slight clicking noise when hooking your release to a metal loop.

Various styles of mechanical releases are available, but they fall into two basic categories — wrist strap and T-handle releases.

Wrist-strap releases are the most common used by bowhunters, partly because they can be strapped on and you always know where they are. Typically, they consist of a short shaft with a set of caliper jaws and a trigger mechanism attached to a wrist strap secured with either Velcro or a buckle. High-end models can be adjusted for trigger pull and most can be adjusted for overall length.

Virtually all wrist-strap releases, even the glove style, are triggered by the index finger after the jaws are clamped over the bowstring or string loop. Some jaws are designed to be open until cocked, and others open with a pull of the trigger and

These two releases are examples of wrist-strap trigger-finger releases, by far the most popular type for bowhunters. The biggest advantage is always knowing where your release is – on your hand!

T-handle releases are another option. They're popular with competitive archers and can easily be used for hunting, too. The important thing is to get used to one style of release and always carry a spare.

then close again when you release. Some have jaws designed to attach to the bowstring, and some have small hooks that slip into a string loop. Still others have double jaws for attaching to the bowstring on both sides of the arrow nock.

Since I hunt almost exclusively with a string loop, I prefer a caliper release with jaws designed for string loops. I also prefer a release with jaws that open when I press the trigger and close when I let up. That allows me to clip on fast when the heat is on.

T-handle releases are also popular with some bowhunters. Those who combine competitive archery with their bowhunting often choose this style release, because they don't want to switch from one style to another when hunting season arrives, a good idea. Such drastic changes in equipment should never be made just before a hunt.

T-handle releases are precision devices with a lot of adjustability. They can be operated by your thumb, middle finger, little finger, or even using back tension (more on that later). Picking up an unfamiliar release is going to feel very odd at first, but as with any change in equipment, you should resist the temptation to go back to your old standby and give the new style a fair shot. Shoot at least a hundred arrows before you decide a release is or isn't for you.

It's not necessary to spend $100 or $200 on a release, unless you're a serious competitive archer. The game animals we hunt care nothing about how much our

QUICK TIPS

- Some finger tabs have slippery calf hair on the surface and a rubber separator to reduce finger pinch. Others have a harder, slicker Cordovan leather surface, and still others feature materials designed to help you maintain consistency in your grip of the string. Check out Three Rivers Archery Supply and choose what works for you, there are no rules.

- If you shoot a mechanical release, always, and I mean always, have two in your possession when hunting. It's not that hard to lose a release, or drop it out of a tree, and they can fail, even something as simple as getting jammed with mud. I keep a spare release in my pack in a handy compartment.

- T.R.U. Ball offers several items that might work well for you. The Speed Nok helps align your string and peep, as does their Speed Loop. Both have "fins" that slip inside your nock for a consistent fit.

- For hunting alone, I prefer a release with a wrist strap, and because I hate Velcro with a passion, I have been using a Tru-Fire Hurricane Buckle for several years. It's not an expensive release, but it has been responsible for many deaths and has never failed me. Other excellent wrist-strap releases are made by Carter Enterprises, T.R.U. Ball, Jim Fletcher, Cobra Archery, Winn Archery, Scott Archery, and Copper John.

- Some wrist strap releases are designed so the release mechanism folds back against your wrist or even slips under your cuff. This really cuts down on the clinking and clanking when climbing metal ladders or steps and when handling treestands and decoys.

- T-handle releases are excellent for competitive archery and are used by many bowhunters as well. The disadvantage is having to keep track of the release in a pocket or your hand and not dropping it. Most can be clipped to the string when on stand, but if the trigger is bumped, they fall off. Tie a thin cord to your release so you can slip it over your wrist and keep a spare release handy. Some excellent T-handle releases for hunting are made by Carter Enterprises, Tru-Fire, T.R.U. Ball, Scott Archery, Spot Hogg, Stanislawski, and Copper John.

equipment costs, and they're the only critics we're worried about in this book. Read that last sentence again and remember it.

Some of the more expensive T-handle releases have triggers that adjust for both travel and tension (I advise against a hair trigger for hunting), and thumb triggers can be configured for a custom fit. To be honest, such releases are designed for the target archer and are overkill for the bowhunter. Then again, if you're both a target archer and a bowhunter, you will probably want a "crossover" release so you can maintain a comfort level from bow to bow.

Finally, there's the back-tension release. Designed to help archers who suffer from "target panic" (oops, there I said it again) these releases are activated by the act of tightening your back muscles and causing a slight "rollover" in your release, triggering the sear. You put your pin in the bull's-eye and continue to flex your back muscles until the release surprises you by triggering. That's a simplified explanation, but the concept is quite complex.

Most will advise against using a back-tension release for hunting, and I agree. I've heard many horror stories of bowhunters who shoot all summer with a back-tension release and then get in a tense hunting situation and are unable to get the release to go off. It might be because they find themselves in an awkward position that doesn't allow their back-tension technique to work, or they just panic and lose their concentration. When a bull elk is 15 yards away, you don't need to be slowly, consciously squeezing your shoulder blades together and hoping your release will go off soon.

Yes, there are bowhunters, Bowhunter Magazine Editor Dwight Schuh for one, who have success with back-tension releases, but most are highly experienced archers who shoot thousands of arrows, year around, with such releases. It is second nature to them, and it comes easily when hunting.

Hunting situations are always tense, and my advice is to keep your bowhunting gear and technique as simple as possible. If you develop a case of target panic that threatens your bowhunting, then you might want to work with a back-tension release during the summer to regain mental control. Otherwise, stick to something with a trigger.

As with just about every aspect of archery and bowhunting, there are countless variations to the way things are done. Somebody is always breaking convention and getting away with it. For example, some back-tension releases also have a trigger. You can't imagine all the experimentation that's done in the archery world. However, when you step from the shooting line to the woods and fields, things change. Time is short, distances vary, and you're shooting at an animal with a heartbeat, excellent hearing, and lightning-quick reflexes.

Archery becomes bowhunting, and we all learn that's a whole different ball game.

CHAPTER SEVEN

This pronghorn is flared up, wired to jump and almost saying, "Just try to hit me with an arrow!" Will reducing bow noise help in these situations? The answer is, you never know, so quiet that bow just in case.

Shushing your Bow

It was my first elk hunt with a bow. I was on the north side of Montana's Fort Peck Reservoir, stalking through the junipers, trying to get a shot at a 6x6 bull I watched drop into a draw. The morning sun was bearing down already, and sweat was sliding down my throbbing temples. I was both hot and wired with excitement.

Thinking the bull was further up the draw, I was slipping along as quietly as possible when the sun just disappeared!

I looked toward the east and saw the silhouette of the bull elk standing on the horizon, blocking out the sun!

The bull had been watching me sneak, probably for several yards. I didn't have a rangefinder in those days, so I estimated the distance at 45 yards and slowly raised my bow as I drew.

This was my first experience with the slight hesitation inherent in most elk. If they smell you, it's over. But if they only see you, or only hear you, it's as if they need a secondary confirmation before bolting. This bull could easily see me but was allowing me to draw. I would later use this quirk in elk behavior to help me kill more than a dozen with my bow, but I was about to learn what happens when you provide that secondary confirmation.

As I raised my bow, the feathers on the foremost arrow in my bow quiver rustled against a twig on a bush in front of me. That bull reared up like Roy Roger's horse and was gone before I could finish drawing. To this day, I believe that had I been using plastic vanes I would have gotten that shot off.

The important lesson learned is this: That tiny, almost imperceptible noise "broke the spell." It confirmed the bull's suspicions and overrode his hope that he was invisible. *Time to go!*

Whether a giant whitetail buck is standing motionless below your stand or a grizzly is straddling a moose kill, cautiously sniffing the breeze, the slightest noise will get you in some kind of trouble. You must not break the spell.

Unless it's the call of an incoming bugling elk, or the sound of my arrow hitting his rib cage, I hate noise of any kind when I'm bowhunting (did I mention that already?) I strive for silence in my clothing, boots, treestands, and packs. If it isn't quiet, it doesn't hunt with me, and that includes my hunting buddies.

Foremost in that quest for silence is a quiet bow, both before and after the shot. But first, let's get another argument out of the way.

Can you make your bow silent? No. Will a big game animal always hear your bow going off? Yes, unless there is distance, wind, rain, or running water to cover the sound.

The speed of sound at sea level and 70 degrees is 1,128 feet per second. That's four or fives times faster than your arrow, meaning the *twang* of your bow will always reach a game animal well before the arrow. Most animals react to that sound rather than the impact of the arrow. That critter has no concept of what an arrow is or what just happened. All it knows is it heard a scary noise, or something hit it, *so run!*

Complicating this debate is the infinitely varying situations and attitudes of individual animals. Is the scene quiet and calm? Is the animal? Is the shot long or short? Does your arrow fly at 180 feet per second or 320? Is the animal aware of your presence? Does it recognize danger? Is it an ultra-quick impala or a less-reactive bull moose? Will a loud bow spook game worse than a quiet one? Does it make a difference? Not all these questions can be answered.

The bottom line is you never want to break the spell by making noise of any type or amplitude, before or after the arrow is launched. So, the singular answer to those questions, at least for the detail-oriented bowhunter, is to get your bow as quiet as possible, just in case.

Something as simple and small as these String Leeches goes a long way toward reducing vibration and noise in both your bowstring and buss cables.

THE TWANG

No doubt, the most significant noise generator on any bow is the bowstring and/or buss cables. Slow-motion video of bowstrings and cables shows an incredible amount of oscillation that seems to go on forever but actually only lasts fractions of a second.

Bow manufacturers have gone to great lengths to reduce and dampen that vibration. Mathews employs their String Suppressors, Hoyt has added their StealthShot String Suppression System, BowTech has a new ShortStop suppression device and Browning uses SRS (String Recoil Suppressor) devices on their Illusion bow.

Aftermarket string suppression systems are also available. They screw into the backside of your threaded stabilizer hole or into the front with an adapter. The business end is positioned up against the bowstring, and they're very effective in dampening string vibration. Four good options are the String Tamer from Norway Industries, the Custom String Suppressor by Meanv Archery, the Shock Terminator Suppressor by STS Archery, and the Rattler from Falcon Products.

One of the biggest names in noise suppression is Sims Vibration Laboratory.

Their products constructed of NAVCOM (Noise and Vibration Control Material) are very popular, and many bow manufacturers include Sim's String Leeches with their bows. These small-yet-effective devices go a long way toward taming the oscillation of your bowstring.

BowJax, Inc., is another manufacturer of products useful in the reduction of bowstring noise. Their string dampeners can be inserted between the strands of your string and/or cables, or slipped over the bowstring after putting your bow in a press.

Two more factors will affect the noise your bowstring generates. If your bow is set at or near its maximum draw weight, it'll be quieter than if set at a lower poundage, when there is less tension on the cables and string.

Shooting a lightweight arrow will also make your bow louder. Typically, the heavier the arrow, the quieter the bow. That's because a heavier arrow absorbs more energy, leaving less behind for the bow and strings to soak up. A poorly tuned bow will also be noisier than one that's set up well.

THE BOW FRAME

We've done what we can to dampen string oscillation, but we've only just begun to make our bow as quiet as possible.

The next step, though there's no particular order, is to soak up the vibration of

A stabilizer will dampen both noise and vibration, but choose one that's not too large and bulky. Note other silencing products including string silencers, adhesive fleece, string suppressor and vibration dampeners built into the bow's riser and a bowsight.

the bow frame. Since Mathews installed Harmonic Dampeners on their bow risers, others have joined the quest to deaden what is essentially an aluminum "tuning fork" holding your limbs in place. If a bow maker hasn't developed their own riser dampening products, like Hoyt's RizerShox, they probably include products from other companies.

To some extent, adding weight to your bow helps, because there's less vibration in a heavy object. That was the original purpose of a stabilizer. Today, stabilizers have become high-tech devices filled with various substances, or engineered in some way that will increase their ability to reduce vibration and noise without adding excess weight.

The options are many in the stabilizer market. Sims' S-Coil Stabilizer is actually quite light, but the integrated NAVCOM material absorbs shock. Another top stabilizer is the Doinker, which features proprietary ITP (Interrupted Transfer Polymer) technology.

Other quality stabilizers that will get the job done are made by Fuse Accessories, Alpine Archery, BowTech, Carolina Archery Products, Vibracheck, TruGlo, NAP, Carbon Express, and Stealth Archery.

If you don't believe stabilizers are beneficial, screw one on your bow and shoot a couple hundred arrows, then take it off. You'll notice the difference. I prefer a stabilizer in the six-inch range, because it's big enough to make a difference yet isn't cumbersome.

Next on the list of vibration sources are your bow's limbs. Parallel limbs and new cam designs have reduced limb travel, which helps cut down on vibration and noise.

You may still find it necessary to add aftermarket limb-dampening devices, such as Sim's Limbsaver Ultra, or BowJax's Monsterjax (or Slimjax for narrow limb bows). Some bow manufacturers have their own designs, including Hoyt's AlphaShox for their split limbs. Martin Archery and Alpine Archery have their own limb dampeners and Horton Vertical offers their Tunerz, a tunable dampener for your limbs and other bow parts.

Still other products can be added to your bow's frame to soak up vibration. Small, stick-on Mini Limbsavers can deaden the vibration of quiver hoods, sights, and other parts. The process requires a bit of experimentation to maximize noise reduction. Each bow responds differently, and what works for one may not work for another.

QUICK TIPS

- **If you hear even the slightest rattling sound when you shoot your bow, take the time to thump the limbs with the heel of your hand, or tap on every accessory, screw, or bolt to see if it's loose. Tighten everything and shoot again, then keep thumping or changing accessories until all the rattling is gone.**

- Quiver hoods are notorious noise-makers, so check all the bolts, screws, and even rivets that hold the hood on the bracket.
- If excessive string noise persists, try installing Sims String Leeches or similar devices in the buss cables as well as the bowstring. Sometimes that's enough to tame the vibration.
- Dirt and gunk trapped under your cable guard slide can make the slide chatter and create noise. Remove the slide and clean both it and the rod from time to time, but don't use any sort of lubricant that can attract grime. Switching to a Teflon slide can help.
- String silencers come in many forms from yarn to rubber "catwhiskers" and other doodads, and even muskox fur. All will quiet your bowstring to some degree, but I'd recommend one that doesn't hold moisture or burrs.
- One of the worst obstacles to a quiet bow is the rubber cord on peep sights. They contribute to the twang of your bow, and that's one reason I don't use them (see Chapter 4).

PRE-SHOT NOISE

You can't totally eliminate the noise created by a released bowstring, but you can kill those nasty "pre-shot" noises, which are far more likely to leave you eating "tag salad" at the end of the season.

Your best tool for this crucial task is adhesive fleece. I love the stuff.

To begin with, place adhesive fleece on any part of your bow that could create a noise. Put a couple strips on the bottom of your upper limb, near the cam/idler wheel, so it doesn't clink when hanging your bow on a hanger. If you plan to do some bellycrawling in rocky terrain, put some fleece on the metal parts of your bow that may contact rocks as you lay the bow in front of you.

Fill your bow quiver with arrows and check to see if your shafts contact parts of your arrow rest or sight. If it's even close, put some fleece on those parts to eliminate vibration as well as those noises that might occur when you remove an arrow.

Next, snap an arrow onto the string and move it around the rest, riser, and shelf in every conceivable position. If there's any contact with metal parts, even the bottom of the sight guard, cover it with fleece. Always line your riser and shelf with fleece, making sure to come over the lip of the shelf. This can prevent "breaking the spell" when hurried to load an arrow.

If you use a Whisker Biscuit with the Quick Shot feature (gap for side-loading an arrow) place a strip of fleece on the rim of the Biscuit, near the mouth of the gap, in each direction. That will prevent a *clink* if you miss the gap with your arrow.

If you use a drop-away rest with a launcher that contacts the shelf, place a thin piece of rubber, then one or two layers of adhesive fleece, at the contact point to silence the collision between the launcher and the shelf.

I absolutely will not tolerate even the slightest noise when I draw an arrow across my arrow rest. There is no more critical moment in bowhunting, and the tiniest noise can break the spell. My launcher is always covered with fleece for a deadly silent draw.

Some good sources of adhesive fleece and other bow-silencing products are CirCut Archery, The Bohning Company, and Hunter's Specialties.

Of course, your bow can make other noises such as creaks and groans when you draw. Possible causes are dirt and grime on the axles or in limb pockets, string yoke attachment points, and even cracked limbs. If your bow makes any sort of noise when you draw, eliminate it, even if that means taking the bow to an archery pro shop to find the source of the noise.

Adhesive fleece is your friend. Nock an arrow and seek any place where it could clink on metal and cover it with fleece. Note fleece on bottom of sight guard.

As you probably realize by now, much effort goes into silencing a bow. Even traditional archers take every reasonable measure to silence their already quiet bows. Does it make a difference? In my judgment, yes, it does in certain hunting situations. Since you cannot predict when you and your bow will be thrust into one of those situations, *shushing* your bow certainly makes good bowhunting sense.

CHAPTER EIGHT

This is a gruesome-looking broadhead wound, but death is never pretty. The only negative to an entrance hole like this is the difficulty in cleaning the animal up for photos afterward. Shoot the most devastating broadhead you possibly can.

Debating Broadheads

Nothing creates friction between bowhunters like the topic of broadheads. What fuels those fires of controversy is the fact that no one is right. Why? Because nothing can be proven to scientific standards.

Even if you have a herd of cloned deer, all the same weight, height, and body structure and could train them to stand in exactly the same posture and angle, you still could not possibly replicate two shots with the various broadheads. It's simply impossible to conduct a real-life, scientific test for penetration, hemorrhaging, and other performance attributes.

Countless unscientific tests have been performed on broadheads, from shooting them through plywood, tires, foam targets, beef rib cages, cement blocks to even high-tech ballistic gel. But, until someone finds a moving, reactive target with thick fur and elastic skin wrapped around a cage of bone and filled with mushy organs and viscous lubricating fluids, any sort of penetration test will be more supposition than science.

While one broadhead design may crash through plywood, another will come apart, but that says nothing about how each will perform when punching through heavy, hollow moose fur, inch-thick skin, a rib the size of a hockey stick, and two feet of warm, wet, squishy air-filled lungs. Neither plywood, nor any other substance, comes anywhere close to the real thing.

Sadly, game recovery problems are often blamed on the broadhead, when shot placement — the single most critical factor in killing an animal with an arrow — was really the culprit. We don't always see what we thought we saw.

Ask any guide who has helped track hundreds of animals. They'll tell you the client's memory and description of the angle and his shot placement is seldom confirmed by reality.

The shot happens in the blink of an eye, and it's difficult to remember precisely what happened. We tend to see what we want to see, and sometimes "great shots" are in fact, something less. It's usually caused by the animal bolting at the sound of the bow, or even just prior to the shot, and that movement can do strange things to an arrow's flight path, even if it does hit the "goodie box."

Unfortunately, we don't often get the opportunity to conduct a thorough necropsy on unrecovered game, but when it does happen, shot placement, not broadhead performance, is invariably the cause. Bad shots happen to us all, sooner or later.

So, what criteria do we use when choosing a broadhead?

The very first and most important quality is sharpness. Not "okay" or "good enough" sharpness. Not mill bastard file sharpness. Not last year's blade sharpness, either. The blades on your broadheads, regardless of design, should be so sharp

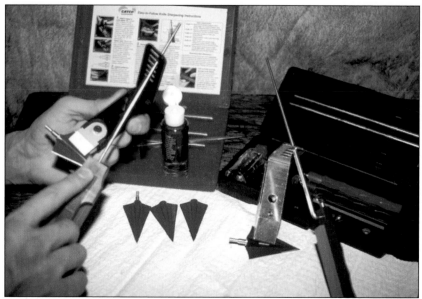

Sharpening your own traditional-style broadheads can be both frustrating and satisfying. Using a sharpening system like the Lansky or Gatco worked for me.

they cut your eyelashes just looking at them. So sharp you're scared to touch them. So sharp that every vein or artery they touch bleeds profusely and won't stop, just like your face after you've shaved with a new blade.

Accept nothing less.

And don't allow your blades to touch anything before they plunge into the quarry you seek. Practice with dull blades, then install virgin blades before hunting, and be very careful when putting broadheads in your quiver, so they don't touch anything in there, either. This is important, because that one vein or artery you manage to slice through just may be the one that causes enough hemorrhaging to create a bloodtrail ample enough to end up at your animal.

After all the work you put into your bowhunting, why would you risk a lost animal because you were too lazy or cheap to use new or ultra-sharp broadheads? You owe it to both the animal and yourself.

If you opt for a broadhead that needs to be sharpened, make sure you have the skill, time, and desire to get the job done correctly. I spent years learning to sharpen traditional-style Zwickey broadheads. By September, my left arm was always bald because I'd shaved all the hair off while sitting in front of the television with a Lansky or Gatco sharpener and a box full of Zwickeys. I was able to get them scary sharp, and they served me well over the years.

There was great satisfaction in taking animals with broadheads I sharpened myself, but my bows got faster and time got shorter, so I went to replaceable-blade heads. Now I'm guaranteed to have razor-sharp broadheads with no effort other than installing fresh blades before every hunt.

Now, to broadhead choice. All well-built, ultra-sharp broadheads will get the job done when you slip an arrow between the ribs and cause a bilateral pneumothorax, otherwise known as a double-lung hit. The lungs collapse and death is actually quicker than with a sudden lose of blood pressure, or massive exsanquination, such as occurs with a heart shot.

Because we don't always make a perfect shot, here's my broadhead philosophy: Choose a broadhead, not for what it will do when your shot is perfect, but for how it will perform when it isn't.

Your goal should always be two-hole penetration. That means your broadhead should be able to break ribs on medium to large game without coming apart, it should hold up if it has to glance around bone, and it should come out the other side in one piece and still be relatively sharp.

In my opinion, straying away from equipment a bit, the quartering-away shot is overrated. Yes, it's a good shot angle, but your first and best choice is dead broadside, because your chances for an exit hole are greatly increased. With a quartering-away shot, you not only have a greater opportunity to penetrate only one lung, but if you aim at the opposite leg, as you should, there's a good chance your broadhead will lodge in the opposite shoulder and you won't achieve two-hole penetration. Yes, you'll kill the animal, and quickly, but you won't likely have as good a bloodtrail as a broadside shot. If you've ever tried to track a bull elk through thin grass, you'll appreciate ample blood spoor.

For bowhunters shooting light poundage bows, such as youngsters, women, and older bowhunters forced to scale down their draw weight for physical reasons, a fixed-blade, cut-on-contact broadhead is a good choice. Because they're generating lower kinetic energy, a two-bladed head, such as a Magnus Stinger, will slip through deer-sized game easily and penetrate deeply into most other North American game. Even when shooting 50 pounds, it's possible to zip through a grizzly with a well-tuned bow, arrow, and broadhead combination.

Fixed-blade broadheads come in various shapes and sizes. The three on the left are smaller heads designed for fast bows. The top two have replaceable blades. On the right are cut-on-contact fixed-blade heads.

It's not advisable to use mechanical heads, especially those that employ a scissor-type action when open-

I used the Easton Bow Force Mapper to measure the force needed to open various mechanical broadheads. On the left are two examples of rearward-deploying mechanical heads. On the right are some over-the-top models.

ing, if your kinetic energy is low, say 50 ft. lbs. or less. Some energy is lost as the blades impact the animal and fold backwards into place. Granted, that does occur in a split second, and momentum helps overcome that split second of drag, but it does impede penetration when using light arrows and low poundage.

Some of the new broadhead designs with blades that deploy rearward would be better, but the large cut diameters of these heads will also bog down with low kinetic energy.

For bowhunters who shoot average equipment, ie. 60 to 70-pound draw weights and hunting arrows weighing from 350 to 500 grains, most broadheads will work well. Fixed-blade broadheads with replaceable blades have dominated the market for years. They are generally strong, fly well out of a tuned bow, and are always sharp, provided the blades are fresh.

However, switching from shooting field points all summer to large, 125 to 140-grain broadheads often required a complete re-tune of your bow. That created some frustration for bowhunters who didn't really know how to tune their bows.

Then along came mechanical broadheads. They were compact and had a ballistic profile not much different from field points, meaning the average bowhunter could screw them on his arrows and he was ready to go – no muss, no fuss.

Well, not exactly. One problem was the mechanical broadhead craze came along about the same time as ultra-lightweight carbon arrows, and the two didn't mix very well. Bow speeds weren't high enough to compensate for the combination of both low kinetic energy and the energy-draining mechanical designs. Horror stories were rampant.

As bow speeds climbed and carbon arrows became available in heavier weights, the penetration problems eased. Early concerns about "kick out" on quartering shots have been addressed by some manufacturers, and the market has decided which mechanical broadhead designs have survived the war.

Some newer mechanicals require very little energy to deploy, and the Rage broadhead is one example. Their "slip-cam" design means the blades slide rearward with little to no effort, and once deployed they have larger cutting diameters than many fixed-blade heads. I measured the force necessary to open their two-blade version, and it took only three pounds two ounces of pressure.

Three other new broadheads with the same concept are the Trophy Ridge Undertaker, Tru-Fire Switch Blade, and the G5 Outdoor Tekan. The blades on all three of these heads deployed with less than two pounds of force.

I was unable to safely measure the force necessary to open the over-the-top, scissor-back style of broadhead, because I could not replicate live, supple fur and skin. That said, these are deadly broadheads with sufficient energy behind them. Good examples are the NAP Spitfire, Grim Reaper, Rocket Steelhead and others.

In recent years, replaceable-blade broadheads have evolved in response to the mechanical market. Most are now designed with shorter ferrules to maintain straight alignment with arrow shafts and cutting diameters have shrunk to as little as one inch and even smaller. Many fixed-blade broadheads now have a low enough profile that they can hang with a mechanical head when it comes to flight characteristics. There's no concern over whether they'll open in flight or fail to open on impact. Some good ones are the Rocky Mountain Blitz, Muzzy MX4, New Archery Products Crossfire, G5 Outdoors Striker, Slick Trick, and Tight Point Shuttle.

If you're shooting a very fast arrow, say 280 feet per second and above, you may have to stick with a low-profile broadhead, either fixed or mechanical. Fixed-blade heads with cut diameters over one and one-half inches may give you tuning problems, because the larger the blades, the more they act like wings.

If your bow isn't quite so fast, I'd stick with large cut, heavy broadheads in the 125-grain range. Screw them to the tip of a heavy arrow and you'll have lots of kinetic energy and momentum and a deep-penetrating combo. These larger broadheads are available from NAP, Muzzy, G5 Outdoors, and others.

If you plan to hunt very large game such as moose and elk, I'd recommend a fixed-blade head just because you may need every bit of energy to go into creating two-hole penetration. You'll get plenty of argument from those who have taken lots of big critters with mechanicals. Just remember, they're likely using very fast bows and heavier arrows.

The arguments will never be solved, and we all have our standards. As long as your broadheads are scary sharp, I, nor anyone else, should care what broadheads you're shooting. That said, be sure to study your hunting regulations very carefully, because some states do care. As do some outfitters. Because of early problems with mechanicals, some outfitters, even in Africa, won't allow their clients to use certain mechanicals.

QUICK TIPS

- Never shoot broadhead blades you intend to hunt with into anything, including foam targets, prior to your hunt. Your blade edges should touch nothing before they hit fur.
- Don't attempt to sharpen replaceable blades. It's unlikely you'll ever get them as sharp as they need to be, so bite the bullet and purchase fresh blades before any hunt.
- Don't expect too much from your broadhead. It's not intended to crash through an elk scapula or break the leg bone of a moose. It won't bail you out of a bad shot.
- When hunting in windy conditions, such as for pronghorns and caribou, consider a quality mechanical broadhead with a low profile. It will be less affected by crosswinds.
- If you plan to hunt in wet weather, wipe a little cooking oil on your broadheads to protect them from rust. Even stainless steel blades can discolor and oxidize.
- Occasionally switch the arrow you're pulling from your quiver. If you continually pull out the same arrow when setting up for elk or after getting in your treestand, the broadhead on that shaft will lose some of its sharpness.
- Monitor your mechanical broadheads both in the quiver and on the end of your arrow to make sure a blade hasn't

Now, let's talk broadhead flight. If a broadhead is well-built, balanced, symmetrical, not overly large, the same weight as your field points, and it's screwed into the right arrow with some rotation built into the fletching (see Chapter 2), it should fly well out of your bow. If it doesn't, don't blame the broadhead.

More than likely your bow is at fault because it's not well tuned. Field points will sometimes appear to fly well out of a poorly-tuned bow, but once you screw a set of wings (your broadhead) to the front of your arrow, you'll find out if your bow is in tune. Any flight anomalies, such as fishtailing, porpoising, or borderline arrow spine, will be amplified by a broadhead, and the bigger the broadhead, the more significant the effect.

Your arrow, whether it's tipped with a field point or a broadhead, should always fly with what I call "invisibility." In other words, you should never see anything but the end of the nock and spinning fletching. If you notice the slightest wiggle or waggle in your arrow at any point in its flight, your set up needs work.

It takes more work to get broadheads shooting well, which is precisely why mechanical broadheads were so quickly accepted. They flew like field points, so some hunters just screwed them on and went hunting. The real problem wasn't solved, but rather ignored. Of course, whatever fixed-blade broadhead they tried popped open. Otherwise, you'll miss.

- Any broadhead, whether fixed-blade or mechanical, with a large cutting diameter of over one and one-half inches will require sufficient kinetic energy to achieve two-hole penetration. Be sure you're using enough draw weight and arrow mass to get the job done.

- For traveling, I like to make a special broadhead case. Anything that keeps your broadheads from rattling and getting dull will work. I have one I made with a Tupperware container and strips of foam that compress the broadheads, keeping them safe and sharp.

- Penetration is greatly affected by arrow flight. A perfectly tuned arrow shot from a 50-pound recurve will zip through a bull moose, while an erratically flying arrow from a 70-pound compound may not penetrate a deer. First things first — tune your bow!

- Always perform a necropsy on the animals you kill. Find out what organs you hit, check the entrance and exit holes, examine your broadhead after the shot, and be objective. Did your broadhead do its job and does it deserve your confidence? This process is also invaluable in helping you understand game anatomy and how to react to specific shots you might make in the future.

prior to the switch was labeled a poor flyer.

Tuning a bow is a big part of this game. Refer back to Chapter 3, which includes a description of broadhead tuning. Another great source of information on tuning a bow is Easton's Tuning Guide, which can be downloaded from their website.

Don't get too worked up about the broadhead debate. I don't. As long as my broadheads are scary sharp and my arrow is flying with invisibility, I'm a happy bowhunter. You should be, too.

CHAPTER NINE

Optics are your eyes to the world. Larry D. Jones and I relied on our high-quality optics to pick out the antlers of bedded red stags in the mountains of New Zealand. If you're serious about hunting, you'll eventually own top-quality glass.

Seeing and Finding Your Way

Don't you get tired of hearing, "You get what you pay for," when it comes to optics? It's a cliché that's reached the annoying stage. Trouble is, most clichés have endured because they're, well, true.

That old cliché was never truer than on a North Dakota mule deer hunt a few years back. I was lying on my belly on the lip of a canyon in the Badlands, glassing for a muley buck I knew was there – somewhere. The rising sun was still low and in my face as I was trying to penetrate deep shadows in a distant draw. It was a long way off, but I kept picking away, searching for the antlers of the buck, which was almost certainly already bedded.

The 10x42 Swarovski EL binoculars pressed against my eye sockets were worth their weight in gold. Despite the flare of the low sun and the black shadows, I was still able to dissect each and every bush and pocket where the buck could be hiding. Lesser glass would have been hazy, and all the branches would have looked like antlers.

I was able to finally locate the buck because I could actually discern the slight webbing in an antler fork, something branches don't have. Slowly, I picked out more antler, then an ear and even an outstretched hind leg.

Now that I knew precisely where the buck was bedded, I began to study the surrounding terrain, looking for other deer and distinct landmarks I could use to reorient myself once I got close. Nothing ever looks the same once you get there, so a mental map is a must.

To make a long story short, I was able to stalk, mostly on my belly, to within 11 yards of that buck, but he was in a deep, worn-out bed and offered no shot. I got impatient and attempted to get him up by throwing a rock, and he bolted.

My impatience cost me that buck, but quality optics got me there in the first place. I seriously doubt I'd have picked out that webbed antler with cheap glass.

Bowhunt long enough, in a variety of terrains, and you'll eventually end up with quality glass. You might rely on poor quality binoculars for a few years, as you collect other primary gear, but sooner or later the logic and the money will make sense. It hurts to pay big money for binoculars, but they become a lifelong investment and a cherished piece of hunting gear you'll never hunt without.

Do you have to spend $1,500 on a pair of binoculars to be a successful bowhunter? Certainly not, but it helps.

Much depends on your type of hunting. If you're a whitetail hunter spending most of your time in a treestand or ground blind, you probably don't need a high-

The type of hunting you do dictates the size of your binoculars. Each size has its advantages and disadvantages. These Leicas have 20mm objective lenses, the Swarovskis, 32mm, and the Nikons, 42mm.

grade pair of 10 power binoculars. A pair of 8x42s or even the smaller 8x32s, might be all you need to spot incoming deer and evaluate antlers.

I hate surprises and strive to see incoming game at the earliest possible moment. The sooner I spot an incoming whitetail, the quicker I get my feet in position, grab my bow, and get settled before the animal gets close. I apply this philosophy whether I'm hunting whitetails from a tree or elk on the ground.

An early warning also helps you ready a grunt call or rattling antlers and gives you time to watch the reaction of the animal. Everything you can learn about game and their reaction to stimuli is valuable. Without binoculars, you're hunting blind.

If your hunting is more complex and involves spot-and-stalk, your optics choice will be affected by the "spot" in that equation. When glassing for muleys, antelope, sheep, or whatever, you could spend many consecutive hours behind your optics. Poor glass can cause eye strain and headaches. Good optics can even reduce wear and tear on the rest of your body by saving you miles of walking. Quality binoculars are actually a weapon.

I like a 10x42 binocular for any hunt where I'll have a long-range view of game. Anything higher than 10X is difficult to hand-hold for long periods. If you'll be glassing from a boat, even 10X is tough to hold, but the extra reach is worth it on a caribou hunt, for example. Binoculars made by Zeiss, Leica, Swarovski, and Nikon EDG are all top-grade, with exceptional clarity, and they will gather more light than your naked eye.

On some hunts I prefer mid-sized glasses in the 8x32 or 10x32 range. The smaller objective lens means a smaller, lighter binocular, which I like when using one hand to scan elk timber at close range.

This is not to say you can't get by with a good quality mid-range binocular. Your budget is your budget, and you can find some very good glass in the $400 to $800 range. Look at Nikon, Zeiss, Burris, Leupold, and others. But remember, this is an investment in your hunting future. Don't rely on a $100 pair of binoculars on a $5,000 hunting trip, or even a hunt in the back 40.

As you venture into an optics retailer, with your budget in mind, look over lots of different binoculars. They'll all look good when gazing across a well-lit store. Instead, go to the store near dusk, if possible, and look into the low light outdoors. Compare brightness and clarity, and look to see if that clarity goes to the edge of the field of view. How do the ergonomics feel to you? Are the binoculars rubber-armored? If not, they should be, to cut down noise as well as dings. If they're heavy, factor that into your type of hunting.

Much of the above advice can be applied to spotting scopes. However, scopes from the top manufacturers will cost you big bucks, so they're a larger investment in your hunting. The quality is superior, but the average bowhunter isn't going to spend a couple grand on a spotting scope.

I use a scope for my whitetail scouting and for my hunts out west for mule deer and antelope, and up north for caribou and moose. If I ever get to go sheep hunting, which is highly doubtful, a spotting scope would be indispensable for evaluating rams before deciding to hike several miles on a stalk.

Personally, I prefer a spotting scope with a variable-power eyepiece. A fixed 20X is okay, but there are times when I like to zoom-in to discern details. Something in the 15X to 40X range works great. You can get more power, but once you zoom to 30X or so, your view will begin to degrade because of heat waves, shake, and reduced light transmission.

You may also want to consider an angled eyepiece spotting scope. It allows you to keep your head at a 45-degree angle to the line of the scope's sight, which can

Spotting scopes are invaluable for hunting in the wide-open west. Reaching out with your optics can make the difference between just seeing deer and seeing massive antlers on those deer.

save your neck from cramping up, especially when in the field using a scope and tripod. If all you do is glass for whitetails from your pickup seat, a straight eyepiece is best.

QUICK TIPS

- When choosing a binocular, you'll find the technology complex. The size of the objective lens (opposite the end you look into) determines how much light will be gathered. The bigger the objective lens, the brighter the binoculars. Of course, you must factor in the quality of the glass. A high-grade binocular will be brighter than cheap glass, even with a smaller objective lens.

- Binocular design is also important. You'll have to choose either roof prism or porro prism. Roof prism binoculars are generally more compact, better quality, and more expensive, which is why they dominate the market. I use and recommend roof prism binoculars.

- When treestand hunting, hang your binoculars on the tree next to you so you're ready to glass any movement. Don't wait until you see a leg or flick of an ear to dig out your binoculars.

- Some serious western hunters prefer to do their glassing through large, high-power binoculars rather than a spotting scope. Glasses in the 15X range are much easier on the eyes than a spotting scope, because you're using both eyes. When teamed up with a tripod adapter and tripod, these larger binoculars are a very good option.

- Even a whitetail hunter can get good use out of large binoculars in the 12X to 15X range. They're great for scouting, because they're quicker than a spotting scope, easier on your eyes, and you can lay them on the seat of your truck so they're always handy.

- Don't neglect your binoculars when hunting heavy timber. Wear a harness so your glasses are handy, and use them often to scan for legs, antlers, and ears. It's almost like X-ray vision.

- A window mount for your spotting scope is essential for long-range glassing from your vehicle. Some are junk, so get one with a quality head that tightens with a single twist of the handle.

- Always carry a lens cleaning kit with solution and a microfiber cloth. Never clean your lenses with paper, and always blow them clean of dirt and grit before wiping. Scratches are forever. Nikon makes a nice cleaning kit.

- When hunting on the go, wear a binocular harness like the one made by Crooked Horn. It keeps your glasses out of the way yet within easy reach.

- This is a bit off-the-wall, but if you get a sliver or something imbedded in your carcass, flip your binoculars around and look through the objective lenses and focus tightly. It will give you an excellent view of your problem.

If the ultimate in low-light vision is your goal, go with the largest objective lens possible. For example, Nikon offers three sizes—50, 65 and 85mm spotting scopes. The larger the objective lens, the better the low-light performance. The companies mentioned also make high-quality spotting scopes, but you can spend less money for scopes from Vortex, Bushnell, and Vanguard. The options are many, so do your research.

To get the most from your spotting scope, you'll need a good tripod. You'll find tripods to fit every budget, from $500 carbon-fiber tripods to $50 economy models. Whatever you spend, choose a lightweight, compact tripod that you'll be willing to carry with you. Slik, Gitzo, and Bogen make top-quality pack tripods that'll set you back some serious cash. Unless you demand the best, you can get a decent tripod for a hundred bucks. Just make sure it's compact enough to carry. Most compact tripods won't extend high enough to use standing up, but that's just a trade-off you'll have to make.

Estimating yardage is a learned skill that's almost impossible at ground level or across open draws. A laser rangefinder is indispensable when having to make a tough shot.

I have a short Slik Carbon tripod with a ball head from a camera supplier called Really Right Stuff. My ball head is designed for photography, and you might prefer a head that pans, or one with a trigger lock. Some high-grade heads are made by Bogen and Jim White, but you can get by with cheaper versions. They just won't be as solid, lightweight, or durable.

RANGEFINDERS

The final weapon in our optics arsenal is the rangefinder. While hunting red stag on New Zealand's South Island in 2007, I slipped up to the crest of a grassy knoll, looking for a good free-range stag I'd been after. The stag spotted me and cameraman Larry D. Jones and took off running, but it helps to have a call inventor behind you. Larry immediately roared at the stag, stopping him cold.

With no time for a rangefinder, I quickly estimated the distance at 40 yards and squeezed the trigger on my release. The stag was probably only 36 yards, and my arrow hit high, severing the spine and dropping the 7x7 in mid-stride. Close enough.

I still practice my yardage estimation skills at 3-D shoots, but have come to depend on my rangefinder. Whether I'm sitting in a whitetail stand or on one knee waiting for a caribou bull to get into range, I'll pull out my rangefinder and range various landmarks, committing those distances to memory. Occasionally, you can range an animal just prior to the shot. I love knowing the exact yardage before coming to full draw.

I once tested all the rangefinders on the market, and when it comes to accuracy there's virtually no difference. Regardless of model or cost, all were accurate to within a yard or so up to 100 yards, and plus-or-minus 3 to 4 yards out to 400 yards.

Accuracy is not a factor, but ergonomics are a major consideration. I prefer the vertically-held rangefinders because they fit nicely in any pocket and can be held steady with one hand against your face. They're also lightweight and inconspicuous.

Avoid a rangefinder with an audible click in the fire button or one that comes with a noisy belt pouch. One rangefinder I tested had a Velcro closure on the pouch! Obviously, that engineer had never spent a day in the field. Watch out for such products. You'll know them when you see them.

Some rangefinders have such good optical quality they can almost double as binoculars. The Swarovski Laser Guide is such a rangefinder, but it will set you back around $800. The Leica is another

Rangefinder technology is improving constantly. They're all equally accurate, but new innovations include angle-compensation technology. The options are many, but choose one based on ergonomics and budget.

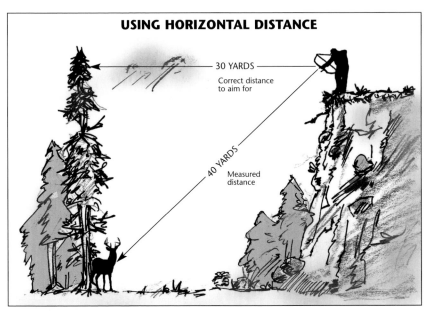

USING HORIZONTAL DISTANCE

30 YARDS
Correct distance to aim for

40 YARDS
Measured distance

When shooting an arrow at sharp downward or upward angles, you need to compensate for gravity, which only acts upon the horizontal distance. An angle-compensating rangefinder will compute the horizontal distance for you, and that's the proper yardage for aiming. Here, you'd use your 30-yard pin.

QUICK TIPS

- When choosing a rangefinder, test it to see if it will acquire a range when the laser is fired through the see/shoot-through netting of a ground blind. Some will; some won't. Only you know if that's an issue.

- Find a good way to carry your rangefinder. Some are happy with just the cord around their neck and the rangefinder in their jacket's breast pocket. Some like belt pouches and other like retractable tethers. Another option is a device made by Cherry Hill Outdoors called the Fast Draw Rangefinder Holder. It clips to you binocular harness strap, or elsewhere, and keeps your rangefinder tethered and handy.

- Always carry spare batteries for your rangefinder. Some are hard on batteries, some are not. I've been using a Nikon Monarch 800 and no matter how hard I try, I can't wear the battery down on that thing.

- Keep your rangefinder lenses clean and be sure to set the focus on the eyepiece (if possible) so you have a sharp image at the ranges at which you'll typically be firing the laser.
- When the day's hunt is over, I always stash my rangefinder in my pack because I never go anywhere without it, and I know I'll never leave my rangefinder behind.

rangefinder with quality optics that excel in low light. Both those brands use red LED displays. Others, like the Nikon, Bushnell, and Leupold models, use black LCD displays, and you'll have to decide which you like best.

The latest technology in rangefinders is angle compensation. Built-in inclinometers determine the angle of the shot, then compute the compensated yardage.

Keep in mind, gravity only applies to the horizontal distance, regardless of whether you're shooting uphill or downhill. For this reason, you'll shoot high on significantly angled shots. To illustrate, think of a tall pine tree standing next to the mule deer buck you're about to shoot at a sharp downward angle. If you range the tree trunk in front of you, horizontally, that would be the yardage you shoot (see diagram).

Opti-Logic pioneered this technology for rangefinders, and now Bushnell, Leupold, and Nikon have angle-compensation rangefinders. If you expect to shoot long uphill or downhill shots, you'd do well to invest in such a rangefinder.

A GPS can be used to mark any location that might be important, such as this obviously well-used elk wallow. I mark such spots whether I plan to come back or not. You never know when your plans might change.

GPS UNITS

When global positioning system (GPS) units first hit the hunting scene, I found myself testing one in Montana's Crazy Mountains. I was hiking back to camp one evening and broke out my new GPS and got a satellite lock. It indicated camp, which I had saved as a waypoint earlier, was about two-tenths of a mile due west. It was wrong. It had to be. There was no way camp was just over the ridge in the next draw. I was certain the GPS was wrong and would have quickly thrown down a $100 wager the gadget was having some sort of technical difficulty.

Nope. I was wrong. I walked over the hill and there was camp. I was flabbergasted. A GPS unit doesn't lie. You might be using it incorrectly, but it knows its stuff.

After evolving from military use to civilian navigation, GPS has become valuable to the hunter for myriad uses. GPS allows you to lock in waypoints to all your treestand sites, elk wallows, antelope blinds, or anywhere you have to go, daylight or dark. I've used them to mark my truck, camp, significant landmarks, forks in the trail, and downed animals. If you need to find some thing or some place again, GPS will make it so.

GPS technology is also surging, and you'll get a headache trying to figure out which unit is best. Look for the one with software that's easy to navigate, then study your owner's manual and practice. It's not as difficult as it seems.

The confidence you get from a GPS when hunting unfamiliar ground is its greatest benefit. With the waypoint of your vehicle's location stored in your GPS, it's much more comforting to take off hunting knowing you can find your truck in the dark, even if you take a different route back! That keeps me hunting fresh ground and keeps me in the "hot zone" right up to the end of shooting light, rather than hoofing it back just before dark. Those extra minutes of prime time, at either end of the day, are precious.

The cost of GPS has gone down in recent years, and you can get a good, serviceable model for a hundred bucks. Some excellent brands are Magellan, Lowrance, and Garmin. Technology in this arena is exploding, and Bushnell has a new unit that layers satellite images, aerial photos, and topographic maps on the screen! There are far too many features and options to list here, so you'll have to do some research of your own to determine which unit fits your needs.

Once you've chosen a GPS, I recommend you convert your unit to UTM, or Universal Transverse Mercator, mode. Most units offer the option with several clicks.

QUICK TIPS

- When shopping for a GPS unit, look for user-friendly software. Have the salesperson demonstrate its use and note how complicated the software navigation is. Most units have far more technology than you'll use, which makes them seem more complicated than they really are. It won't take long to learn to use a GPS and experimenting while riding in a car helps.

- As you hunt high country, for example, take waypoints at various points along the way. If you're hunting with a buddy you can split up, maximizing your hunting, and meet back at any predetermined waypoint you've saved.

- It's easy to direct your hunting buddy to a great hunting spot you've located just by giving him your GPS coordinates. He inputs the coordinates into his unit and the GPS will take him directly to the spot.

- When searching for downed game, and the trail goes cold, I set my GPS to plotter trail so I have a visual map of where I've been. I can work a grid search and actually see where I've been and where I haven't. This is extremely valuable in the dark when it's easy to get turned around.

- Most units contain sunrise/sunset tables, moon phases, and some predict hourly game and fish activity according to lunar phase. Even if you don't believe in such things, it's fun to note whether the predictions are accurate.

- The act of using a GPS, which gives you bearing and track in compass degrees, will help you better understand how to use a compass and topo maps. Most higher end GPS units can be loaded with topographical maps, which can be easily navigated.

- A GPS is very useful, even in the midst of civilization. Store and share waypoints for your home, gas stations, restaurants, airports, lodges, and any place you might meet hunting buddies while traveling. In emergencies you can even provide a waypoint to rescuers.

When looking at a topographic map, latitude and longitude are virtually useless to most of us. UTM aligns your GPS unit with the grid format used by the U.S. Geological Survey on topographical maps. Provided, of course, your maps feature the UTM grids (widely available) which are one kilometer square. It will require a learning curve, but in a nutshell, it's much easier if your GPS indicates your elk wallow is 450 meters on a bearing of 60 degrees. Latitude and longitude mean virtually nothing to a bowhunter.

Let me put it another way. Instead of the traditional GPS format merely telling you how to get to places you've already been, UTM allows you to pick any spot on a detailed map and navigate to it with exceptional accuracy. Once you learn UTM, you'll never go back.

Of course, you never, ever want to rely solely on any electronic device for navigation. You'll still want a compass in your pack and, just as importantly, a good map. Maps aren't just for survival either. With experience, you can look at a topographic map and pick out potential bedding areas, pinch points, waterholes, and other game-attracting landmarks and plan your hunt accordingly.

There are several sources for topographic maps, including the U.S. Geological Survey, and the best way to contact them is through their Internet site at http://topomaps.usgs.gov/. Internet sites that offer custom maps of all types include www.topozone.com and www.mytopo.com.

OTHER SCOUTING TOOLS

There are a number of other tools that will help you scout for game, and one is the trail camera. The technology sweeping through this industry contains a tidal wave of information I won't get into too deeply here. Trail cameras are excellent tools for answering the when, where, and what questions in your scouting efforts. Just knowing what kind of animals are roaming your hunting ground is a huge benefit and can increase your resolve when it comes to holding off and waiting for The Big Dog.

Trail cameras can give you strong resolve to hold out for a big buck, if you've actually seen evidence the animal exists. They also add a degree of entertainment to your scouting efforts.

The options are staggering, ranging from a simple camera strapped to a tree to motion-activated video cameras and still cameras that will instantly send images to your cell phone anywhere in the world! Even the Pope and Young Club has expressed concern about the fair chase aspects of some of the new cameras. What if you get a cell phone message with an image of a buck that just walked past a nearby camera and you were able to move to an intercept position? Is a line being crossed?

Functionally, some users of trail cameras feel the flash of the camera on night photos tends to spook game, particularly mature whitetail bucks. Whether or not flash spooks game remains a debate. Here's a story that doesn't solve it either.

I was sitting in a Double Bull ground blind in Saskatchewan a couple years ago when a 120-class whitetail buck walked into bow range. The outfitter had forgotten to turn off his trail camera, and it flashed in the buck's face from about five feet away. He did not react. No flinch, nothing. Minutes later, he walked back in the direction he came from and it flashed again. This time he flinched slightly, then calmed down. Granted, it was daylight, so the flash wasn't bright, and this was not a crafty old mature buck, but he barely noticed the flash. On the other hand, some hunters report fewer and fewer images the longer a flash camera is in place. The debate continues.

In response to this dilemma, trail camera makers offer infra-red cameras that don't use flash. They take color daytime photos and black-and-white nighttime images without flash. Consumers seem more comfortable with this option when it comes to spooking game.

Digital cameras have taken over the market, because there's no film to develop and you can get instant viewing of images. Also, when using large capacity memory cards, hundreds of images can be stored between visits when cards can be changed out.

If I were buying a trail camera today, I'd stick with the digital, infra-red models. You'll have to do some research and decide how much remote scouting your wallet can stand. Some excellent trail cameras are made by companies such as StealthCam, Cuddeback, Bushnell, Leaf River, Moultrie, and others.

Other tools you can use for scouting are aerial maps available from www.terraserver.com. Zoom in to your favorite hunting spot and have them print an aerial map for you. You can do some pre-hunt strategizing, mark treestand locations, and learn things you didn't know about the area.

If you have access to a small plane, it can be a huge benefit. My buddy has a small tail-dragger, and occasionally we fly over potential hunting grounds during the summer to see what sort of crops are being grown in what areas. We occasionally find little pockets of cover and even spot large, velvet-antlered bucks in places we'd least expect. Any sort of observation technique will help you scout for game.

The best technique, as always, is to get out there, on foot, looking for sign.

CHAPTER TEN

Treestands have changed the game when it comes to bowhunting. Putting yourself above the animal's line of sight is a major advantage in your efforts to get within bow range.

The Treestand Arsenal

Few things have changed the face of bowhunting like treestands. In my home state of North Dakota, treestands were actually illegal until the mid-60s. Sitting in an elevated stand was considered cheating.

To be sure, if we all hunted from ground level, success rates, at least for whitetailed deer, would be considerably lower. Hunting from treestands can put your scent above the noses of game, but more importantly, it gets you above their line of sight, a huge advantage when it comes time to draw your bow.

And treestands are not just for whitetails. Strategically placed treestands are extremely effective when hunting elk, mule deer, Coues deer, and even brown bears. Any time there's good sign next to a tree big enough to hold you, it's potentially a good place to throw up a stand.

One thing you give up when hunting from a treestand is mobility. You're stuck there and can't move with the game, at least not without the commotion of getting down or moving the stand. If the wind switches and blows toward incoming game, you're forced to get down. If animals are passing by out of range, you're out of luck when safely strapped to a tree.

The solution to that problem should be obvious. You need options. That means building a treestand arsenal loaded with likely hunting spots for every season, wind direction, and time of day. Getting away from the rest of your busy life to bowhunt is tough. You can't afford to sit at home because the wind is wrong.

The more options you have, the better decisions you'll make. Hunting your favorite honey hole when the wind isn't right, just because you don't have another choice, is bad bowhunting.

There are three basic treestand types, so let's look at each.

HANG-ONS

Because they're versatile, quiet, and relatively inexpensive, hang-on stands are the most popular option for bowhunters. You can never have too many hang-on stands in your arsenal, and it pays to have a variety.

For run-and-gun hunting, where I slip in and pick a tree, or haul a stand up a mountain to an elk wallow, I like lightweight, low-profile hang-ons. By "low-profile," I mean a stand that folds flat and rides inconspicuously on my back, over the top of my backpack, or under, which usually works better. Lone Wolf treestands are one example of a great run-and-gun stand. Their cast-aluminum construction reduces creaking noises, they fold flat, and they are lightweight.

Summit Treestands makes the Deer Deck and the folding Copperhead, both of which are lightweight and easy to hang. There are others, of course, but you get the idea. One advantage of the Summit stand is you can attach the strap and hanger device to the tree first, then hoist up the stand with a pull rope and quickly hook it up, saving you from having to hold the weight of the stand while adjusting the strap for length.

Now, I'm 6' 5", and when geared up with my 30-lb. pack, I weigh over 250 pounds. I need to be careful about going too light with my stands. I used to prefer treestands held on with chains, but nylon straps have proven to be more than strong enough. I've never had a problem, but then I'm always wearing a safety harness (see Chapter 11) whenever I'm elevated.

Most often, I plan to hang a stand and leave it. In that case, weight and size are not much of a factor in my treestand choice. I opt for comfort, because I'm prone to the insane strategy of sitting in a stand from an hour before dawn until dark, particularly during the whitetail rut. I seldom hunt elk from a treestand, but I have come across wallows and well-used trails in saddles where I would be confident an all-day sit would produce a high-percentage shot.

Large platforms allow me to move my feet around, but the most important feature I seek is a comfortable, quiet seat. As a young bowhunter I used to stand all day, but I don't do that anymore. I need a seat that's easy on my hind end over long hours. A

If your chosen tree is anything but limbless and straight, you'll need a hang-on treestand. Their versatility makes them the favorite of most bowhunters.

thick cushion is nice, and a wide seat allows me to shift my weight from one cheek to the other.

If, like me, you stand frequently to rest your hindquarters and stretch, you'll need a treestand with a seat that folds up and out of the way when you stand. It must also lower back into position easily and do it all in total silence. No squeaks, creaks, or clanks.

For me, another factor is seat height. Most stands have seats in the 19 to 21-inch range, but I prefer a higher seat. If I'm too low it takes more commotion for me to stand up in preparation for a shot. I like a stand with an adjustable seat height, but they're hard to find. One option is the Grizzly Edge II, a two-piece stand with a platform supported by an A-frame brace underneath. It's adaptable to any tree and has a separate seat section that can be set at any height.

I also like treestands that use heavy duty ratchet straps for attaching to the tree. I can crank them down and prevent any movement or slippage of the platform. As the weather gets cold, stands tend to loosen up and get noisy. With a ratchet strap-type stand, you can simply give it another click or two before getting into the stand.

I live in North Dakota, so finding a decent tree to hang a stand in is tough enough. Finding a straight tree adds another dimension of difficulty. That's why I appreciate a hang-on stand that allows me to level the stand platform in crooked trees. The Lone Wolf Assault, Summit Deer Deck and Copperhead Compact, and Gorilla Silverback are examples.

Some hang-on treestands can be adjusted to leaning trees, adding to their versatility. The two-piece stand in this photo can be hung in most trees, and the seat height is adjustable.

Versatility is the key when choosing a portable hang-on stand. Find one that will adjust to the situation, go up easy, and is both secure and silent.

Okay, you can strap a hang-on stand to your back, hike in, pick a tree, and get elevated just as you would with a climber. There's just one big difference. You'll have to consider how you'll get up the tree.

Screw-in tree steps are one way, but there are considerations. In some areas, such as state and/or federal land, screw-in steps may not be allowed. Part of the reason is they can kill trees. I've seen it with some fragile cottonwoods in a Minnesota cane swamp. Trees that I hunted out of would actually start to split at the tree step hole, and I know of two that died and fell over because of my use of tree steps over the years.

Safety is also a consideration with tree steps. If left in over long periods of time they can grow into the tree, get rusty, or even loosen. A hunting buddy of mine had a screw-in step pull out when he was 10 feet off the ground. He broke his leg and had to drag his dangling foot a quarter-mile in the snow before driving himself home. Others have fallen and caught themselves on screw-in steps, and it isn't pretty. Still, I use them often, but I'm especially careful and always maintain three points of contact when climbing.

Strap-on steps are another option. They don't penetrate the bark of a tree but attach by wrapping a strap around the trunk and then cinching tight. There is some give on this type of step, but they work and are safe if you take all the same precautions when climbing.

Climbing ladders or sticks are the best option. They're bulky to carry in, and can be noisy, but if you're careful you can get elevated quickly and safely by strapping them to the tree and working your way up. Two styles are available, independent sections that allow you to adjust to the shape of any tree, and the "stick" style which are assembled as a straight piece, leaned up against the tree and strapped on as you climb.

Independent section systems include Lone Wolf Climbing Sticks, which strap neatly to the stand on your back and are very compact. Summit's Buck Steps allow you to put both feet at the

Strap-on ladders or sectional ladder systems are becoming a favorite way to get elevated. They're somewhat bulky and noisy to get set up, but they're safe and easier to climb, especially in cold weather.

same level, which is very nice when hanging a stand. The Rapid Rails from Non-Typical Treestands and Gorilla's Climbing Sticks are other examples.

Climbing sticks that connect into one piece include Summit's Swiftree Ladder, API's Quik Stik Ladder, Ameristep, Gorilla's Stacking Sticks, Big Game Treestand's Quick Stick XL and River's Edge Rapid Stick. All can be assembled on the ground, then set against the tree. Start by cinching the straps on the bottom section, then work your way up, pull up your stand, set it, and hunt. It looks more complicated and time consuming than it is. Once you have the process down, climbing sticks are an efficient and safe way to get elevated.

QUICK TIPS

- Always wear a safety harness that has a "lineman's" type of safety rope when hanging stands. You can throw the rope around the tree, adjust it for length, and have your hands free for hanging your stand.

- Every time you hang a stand, and before getting into a stand that's been left out, inspect it for damage or problems. A bolt may be loose or a squirrel could have chewed on a strap. Be especially careful if someone else hung the stand. Trust nothing or no one.

- Always make sure your treestand platform is either level or leaning slightly upward at the front. If the platform leans downward, you will constantly feel like you're falling and your body and equilibrium will get a work out.

- Never place a treestand on the back side of a leaning tree. Even a tree that leans a couple degrees toward your back will make you suffer. Place the stand on the up side of the lean or pick a different tree.

- To make my treestands as quiet as possible, and for extra safety, I purchase additional ratchet straps at the hardware store and crank them down hard so the stand really bites into the tree. It also prevents any noisy and unsafe shifting when I move around on the stand.

- Some stands, such as the Gorillas, feature sound-deadening finishes that work great. You can also add camouflage tape to the platform of your stand to help quiet things down.

- For the ultimate in silent movement, place some type of pad or rug, similar to a kitchen rug, on your stand platform. Not only will it quiet your foot movement, but it will help keep your feet off cold metal on those late-season hunts.

- Don't discount a treestand equipped with a foot rest. Resting your boots on that raised bar takes the pressure off the back of your thighs and is a welcome change in position.

- Some trees have very noisy bark when your back or shoulders rub against it. Cover the tree behind you with soft camouflage material. In a pinch, you can even wrap a fleece pullover around the tree behind you, tying off the sleeves.

- If you plan to leave your stand up, be sure to take along a padlock and chain to secure it to the tree. Use a lock designed for outdoor use. It won't deter all thieves, but it will stop those scumbags who don't plan ahead and bring bolt cutters.

- If your stand has shoulder straps or other straps with excess length, make sure you tie the excess off or tighten the straps so they don't flap in the wind and attract attention.

- When using screw-in steps, place them off to the side as much as possible rather than straight up your climbing path. Should you slip and fall, you won't impale yourself.

- To prevent theft of your climbing sticks or ladders, take the bottom section out with you, if possible. You won't stop every thief, just the lazy ones.

CLIMBERS

Personally, I don't have a lot of experience with climbing treestands. I never used one until the last 10 years or so because there just aren't many suitable trees where I live. To use a climber, you need a straight tree without significant limbs and relative consistency with regard to trunk diameter. In the South it's easy to find such trees, and that makes climbers very popular there.

Climbing stands offer several advantages. You can hunt on the fly, choosing a tree near the hottest sign or most-used trail. The first time you hunt any stand location is usually the best, and a climber contributes to that strategy. Climbers also allow you to get as high as your nerve will take you. In the South, where the deer walk around looking up in the sky, bowhunters generally need to get much higher than we do up north.

One thing I like about climbers is I can set the seat at the precise height most comfortable for my long legs. In fact, climbers can be so comfortable it's hard to stay awake! That said, I am nervously slow when using them because of my inexperience. I prefer a climber with a wrap around bar to sit on when climbing. It just gives me a better feeling of security. Climbers I like include the multi-featured Summit Ultimate Viper SS, API's Grand Slam Magnum Extreme, and Gorilla's Greyback Magnum.

Some climbers have small, compact seat sections without guard rails. If you're used to climbers and feel comfortable with this design, they are lighter and more compact, plus you don't have a guard rail in the way of your bow's bottom limb. Good examples are the Lone Wolf Alpha Hand Climber, Summit's Open Shot, and

Getting confidence in a climbing stand takes practice, but these stands are efficient and comfortable when the right trees are available.

QUICK TIPS

- It's absolutely crucial you make certain the rope that connects the two halves of your climber is always in place and cannot come untied. If an un-tethered bottom section should slip off your feet, it could slide to the bottom of the tree, leaving you stranded.

- Using a climbing stand does not exempt you from using a safety harness. I still wear my Seat-O-The-Pants harness with the safety rope around the tree trunk. With each step up, I slide the rope ahead of me. Should something go wrong, I know I won't hit the ground.

- Be careful not to set your seat section so high that when you stand up it's in the way of your bottom limb when shooting.
- Once you're up in the tree, you're stuck there until the hunt is over. Dropping something important can be a problem. Keep an extra release in your pack and you might carry some type of retrieval device with a hook on it. Whatever you do, don't drop your quiver, or you'll have to climb all the way down. Just another reason to stick with a bow quiver!

API's Grand Slam Extreme Bowhunter.

A good compromise is Summit's Razor SS, Loggy Bayou Mega Transformer, or Lone Wolf's Alpha Sit-and-Climb. On these stands the guard rail can be used to sit on when climbing, then dropped out of the way once you're set.

LADDER STANDS

I won't go too deeply into ladder stands, because they're somewhat self-explanatory. Ladder stands are very popular with outfitters because of safety considerations and because hunters of all ages can use them and feel secure. They can be placed in traditionally good locations, such as near food plots or creek crossings, and left for long periods of time. Deer do not notice the ladders any more than a tree branch.

Ladder stands are also comfortable to hunt out of and larger, two-person models are great for taking a young hunter or

Ladder stands are the safest way to get elevated. If you've got a spot that's in the middle of the action year after year, set a ladder stand there and leave it. Be sure to check it for tightness before every use, however.

non-hunting friend or spouse along on a sit.

In the past, ladder stands were dismissed by some hunters because they typically only put you at 15 to 18 feet off the ground. That's not high enough for some bowhunters, so the market responded. Grizzly Treestands (Ameristep) came out with their 22-foot Skyscraper and Big Game Treestands has a 20-footer called the Skybox Deluxe.

Even with a ladder stand you'll need to wear a safety harness, and for all ladder stands and hang-on treestands I recommend a climbing system that helps you stay connected to the tree at all times. Summit's Climbing System is a 30-foot rope that is tied off above your head once the stand is up. The other end is tied off at the bottom of the tree. The clip on your safety harness attaches to a Prussic hitch, which you slide up or down as you climb. As long as you're off the ground, you're safely hooked to the rope.

Any time your feet leave the ground, your brain should instantly think safety!

CHAPTER ELEVEN

Whenever you're elevated, safety must be the first thing on your mind. Note the safety rope around the tree trunk, keeping me safe when hanging a stand. Don't get careless!

Bowhunting Safety

PLEASE – DO NOT SKIP THIS CHAPTER.

Safety is a topic not everyone wants to read about, but in this pursuit we call bowhunting, it's a matter of life and death. There's much more to safety than just wearing a safety harness.

Safe bowhunting begins at home when you're planning your hunting excursions. It doesn't matter if you're walking out your back door to your treestand (you lucky dog!) or flying to the other side of the planet, it's crucial someone knows exactly where you're going and when you'll be back.

I'll refer back to my hunting buddy who broke his leg when a screw-in tree step pulled out (he was only 10 feet off the ground).

He ended up lying in the snow with a boot facing the wrong direction. It was morning, dark, and the temperature was eight degrees. I had my deer already, so he was hunting alone. His wife didn't have a clue where he was and wouldn't start worrying until at least noon. He didn't tell me or anyone else where he was planning to hunt. His cell phone was in his pack, already hanging by his stand! He'd climbed down to unhook his bow, which he couldn't pull up because it was caught on a limb.

Fortunately, his bow was an older, long-axle-to-axle Hoyt, so he was able to use it as a crutch. He began to hobble toward his truck, his foot dangling loose and uncontrollable, when he came to a woven-wire fence. He actually had to throw his discombobulated leg over the fence. He finally made it back to his truck and drove home. He was lucky, if you can call being out of work for months lucky. Had he been unconscious, or unable to move, he'd have frozen to death before anyone found him.

Be certain someone, especially hunting buddies knowledgeable about your hunting area, know where you'll be hunting. Stick to the plan or notify someone of any changes. What could be worse than lying there, helpless and hurting, knowing no one will even know where to look for you?

Another aspect of safety, for which you must plan ahead, is weather. Look ahead at forecasts and beware of incoming fronts, but never bet your life on the accuracy of a forecast. Even with today's technology there's a lot of guesswork in forecasting. Plan for all kinds of weather, both good and bad. Layer your clothing, starting off with a synthetic layer next to your skin (see Chapter 14) and take enough clothing to protect you from hypothermia. Never take chances if there's lightning; head back to your vehicle or camp. Make sure you have survival gear in your vehicle or pack. Always plan for the worst.

QUICK TIPS

- If you have cell service where you hunt, take your phone with you and keep it on your person. However, don't count solely on your phone or any electronic device.

- Name all your treestands and make sure your friends and family know which stand you'll be hunting.

- Get an aerial photo of your hunting area and mark the stand sites and leave copies with someone who knows where you're hunting.

- Take GPS coordinates of your stand or blind sites and add them to your map or leave the list with someone who can pass that information on to searchers.

- In some situations it might be a good idea to leave a note on the seat of your vehicle that is visible from outside and tells searchers which direction you're hunting and other hunt plans.

- Get a whistle and keep it where you can get to it. I've seen some zipper pulls that double as a whistle. Everyone knows to respond quickly to frantic whistling, and it takes very little physical effort on your part to blow a shrill whistle that carries a long way.

- If you're hunting remote country, it's wise to hunt with a buddy so you can keep track of each other. Hunting alone can be dangerous.

When it gets dark, there's no piece of gear more important than some type of light. Whether you're hooking up a safety harness in a dark treestand or hiking through the black night, an LED headlamp, AND a reliable flashlight, are indispensable. And don't forget the extra batteries!

Once your hunt begins, it's very likely you'll be walking around in the dark at some point. Get yourself a quality LED headlamp for hiking in the night. There are various styles, including those that clip on the bill of your cap and lamps with headbands. The LED bulbs are plenty bright to illuminate your path and prevent you from getting poked in the eye or falling off a cliff. They're very easy on batteries, but I always carry spares.

It's also a good idea to carry an extra light, and I usually have a good handheld flashlight with extra batteries along. A Xenon bulb is much brighter and can be used to penetrate the darkness when necessary. The dark woods without a light is a scary place, and I've not seen much evidence a light will spook game.

If you plan to hunt in a treestand, it's imperative you wear a safety harness. Don't bother with the old waist belts or a harness that only wraps around your chest. These devices may keep you from hitting the ground, but you'll likely still get injured and could suffocate. Wear only a full-body safety harness that has leg straps and a tether that extends from the middle of your back. I wear a Seat-O-The-Pants harness whenever I'm elevated, and I wouldn't consider climbing a tree without it. The Hunters Safety System is another excellent harness.

For the ultimate in treestand hunting safety, use a "climbing system." This is a rope that hangs next to your stand and is tied at the bottom. You clip your harness to a Prussic hitch and you're never at risk when climbing.

Also, consider a climbing system rope. These are heavy ropes tied to the tree, top and bottom, with a Prussic hitch that slides up and down the rope. Simply attach your harness tether to the Prussic hitch and slide it as you ascend or descend the tree. You will remain attached at all times, even during the most dangerous moment, when you're transitioning from the steps to the treestand. Summit's Climbing System is excellent.

I've heard every excuse there is to not use a safety harness, and not a single one of them makes any sense. You'll feel strange at first but, like wearing a seat belt, you'll get used to it. If not for you, wear one for your family and the people who might have to find your crumpled body at the bottom of a tree.

Remote hunts are a different animal when it comes to dealing with your personal safety. Help will be hours or days away, and

When hunting wilderness, something as simple as a stumble on a shale slide could snap a leg bone. Always be asking yourself, "What if?"

you can't afford to take chances. I love to hunt alone once in awhile, but not when I'm in remote places. I shot a mountain lion in self-defense years ago and the outcome could have been different.

I was bugling a bull elk from a mountain top and behind me I heard a faint, soft footstep, so faint I almost didn't bother to turn around. When I did, I saw a large tom lion crouched and facing me at 18 yards.

To make a long story short I talked, then yelled, at the big cat, trying to convince him I was a human. He didn't take the hint and took two slow steps toward me, like a housecat stalking a ball of yarn. That's when I knew one of us was going to spill blood, and it had better be me.

Still, I gave the cat the benefit of the doubt by shooting an arrow into the tree next to him. He barely flinched. That was the end of my civility. The second arrow struck him on the side of the throat (a deadfall blocked a shot to the vitals) and he ran off. I tracked him for four and a half hours and finally lost the faint bloodtrail. I shudder to think what would have happened had I not turned around and took off running, like I sometimes do, toward the bull elk. Even just a short wrestling match could have left me dead, or severely wounded, and I was three miles from camp and all alone.

Obviously, you can't predict such scenarios, but if you're in grizzly country you should be taking appropriate precautions such as paying attention, carrying bear spray, or having a back-up weapon where legal.

Even just a sprained ankle in the high country can threaten your life if you have to spend the night in cold weather, risking hypothermia. Be prepared, and always carry a survival kit on such hunts. Such a kit should contain multiple fire starting tools such as lighters, waterproof matches, and magnesium firestarter. You'll also need something to get the fire going, such as a commercial fire starting product, a Ziploc bag full of clothes dryer lint or other flammable material. A mylar survival blanket, or something to build a quick shelter with, is a must. It's also a good idea to carry a rope, knife, whistle, signaling mirror, first-aid kit with Dermabond (super glue for skin), small amount of duct tape wrapped around a pen, pain reliever, trail mix and, of course, some method for purifying or carrying water. Hunts in snow and cold will require a more extensive survival kit.

QUICK TIPS

- A quality first-aid kit is a must, and you should have some basic knowledge of first aid, CPR, Heimlich maneuver, etc. The more you know about stopping bleeding or treating shock, the better hunting partner you are. You could save yourself as well.

- Carry a supply of pain killers that will handle a tough headache or an inflammatory injury. My pack always contains some 800 milligram Motrins (ibuprofen), which will knock down the worst headache or ease back pain. Tylenol (acetaminophen) is fine for a headache, but it won't relieve inflammatory pain.

- If you're hunting at high altitude, say 7,000 feet and above, read up on the symptoms and treatments for altitude sickness. You can take certain medications, such as Diamox, as a preventative measure, but consult your doctor before taking any drugs. If you or your hunting partner get a bad case of altitude sickness, the quickest remedy is to get down the mountain.

- Know where the nearest hospital is and how to get there. In coastal regions, such as Alaska, you can carry a transponder that will signal the U.S. Coast Guard you're in trouble.

- Never walk or run with an arrow nocked or in your hand. I actually watched a bowhunter walk under my stand, on snow-covered ground, with a handful of broadhead-tipped arrows in one hand, his bow over his shoulder! A simple stumble can leave you bleeding profusely and/or dead!

- Keep very close track of your carbon arrows. Check for cracks by flexing them and listening for noises, especially if a particular arrow is subjected to abuse. Also, check your nocks for cracks. Even a tiny crack can cause the equivalent of a dry-fire and your bow could explode in your face.

- Make certain your broadheads are shoved deep enough into your quiver hood that the blades are not exposed. Exposed blades can cut your hands or even your buddy's bowstring if he piles his bow on top of yours.

- Always use a broadhead wrench when installing or removing broadheads. One slip and your season could be over.

- Never shoot a bow with a damaged string. Even if one strand is broken, replace the string immediately.

- Wear safety glasses when cutting arrows, putting your bow in a press, or doing anything that could threaten your eyesight.

- Use extreme caution when field-dressing or caping big game animals, and be sure you wear latex gloves to ward off bacteria and other nasty organisms.

Other safety considerations are borne mostly from common sense, such as always identifying your target and the background. Bowhunters have been killed when a bull elk got between them and arrows flew. Try to anticipate and recognize potential accidents, and get in the habit of asking the question: "What happens if...?"

CHAPTER TWELVE

Black bears are not usually associated with the use of ground blinds, but this big seven-foot boar is one of the only bears I've had come to a bait that didn't know I was there. I shot him from a Double Bull blind only 15 yards away!

Ground Blinding

I'll admit it. I was a little uneasy sitting in a Double Bull ground blind 15 yards from an active black bear bait. The fact my guide had just pointed out two pairs of cub tracks in the shoreline sand not 20 yards to my left didn't help either. If that sow showed up and one of her cubs became curious about the blind and crawled in, my cameraman and I would have a rodeo on our hands.

I considered throwing up a couple treestands instead, but decided to stick with the ground blind approach. Whatever happened, it would be exciting!

Long before the Manitoba sun was even close to the horizon, I caught a flash of black in the bush to my right. My eyes immediately began scanning for cubs. There were none. Just one bear that looked big, and it was headed for the bait.

I really suck at judging black bears, so before getting in the blind I'd cut a slash 36 inches above the ground, in a small tree near the bait. That was my size reference. When the bear got to the bait, and the slash disappeared behind black fur, I came to full draw.

It was early June, and the bears were rutting. This boar was cruising for sows and wasn't interested in the bait. He sniffed around for only a few seconds and was on his way to other parts when I slipped an arrow behind his shoulder.

That seven-foot boar, with a $19^{10}/16$ skull, was the first bear I've ever had close to me that didn't know I was there. Typically, bears know you're in the tree but tolerate your presence because you're in a submissive posture, conceding the bait to them. If you were to attempt to get down, there could be trouble.

As with all ground blind hunting, the excitement is particularly intense due to being eye-level with the animal. That's true when hunting pronghorn antelope, deer, elk, turkeys, whatever. You're up-close-and-personal rather than looking down at them from a treestand.

But that's only one reason ground blind hunting has grown so popular. Another is its effectiveness. Turkeys are oblivious to a ground blind, even in an open field, and pronghorn antelope tolerate a blind very well, even it if hasn't been put up well in advance. Whitetails are less tolerant of a new and strange object. It's often necessary to set a ground blind out in advance, brush it in, and cover the shooting holes with shoot-through mesh before a mature whitetail buck is comfortable around it.

There are three basic types of ground blinds. The natural blind, usually built with available foliage and brush. You can dig in behind a deadfall or pile some leafy branches near thick brush to break your outline. All you need is a saw and a pair of ratchet clippers to make a natural blind.

A "makeshift" blind makes use of some camouflage material or netting as well as natural cover. One effective method is to carry three stakes, some bulk camouflage material, possibly leafy 3-D stuff, and some clips or clothespins of some kind. By pushing the stakes in the ground and arranging the camouflage material in front of you, it's possible to remain hidden, even during that crucial moment when you must draw to shoot. The methods and materials that can be used are countless and dependent on the terrain and available cover.

Finally, we have the increasingly popular pop-up ground blind. I've done quite a bit of hunting from Primos' Double Bull blinds, because they're well-built and constructed in such a way as the walls don't flap in the wind. That can be very important, especially

Regardless of species, it's a good idea to brush a ground blind in or place it where it will be the least noticeable. Note the bait pile in foreground and blind in back.

There are various ways to haul a blind around. In the right kind of terrain a pull golf cart works well. My son Jared is 6' 9" and has size 17 feet, which explains the tennis shoes on this turkey hunt.

on the open, treeless prairie. There are other ground blind manufacturers, such as Ameristep and Eastman Outfitters, and blinds come in various sizes, materials, and designs. All pop up quickly and provide excellent concealment from the wary eyes of game.

Choose a blind made with a camouflage pattern that will blend into the terrain you're hunting. You may still need to brush the blind in, if possible, even if you aren't hunting whitetails.

Next, you'll need to transport your blind, and that can be a trick. Some have shoulder straps on their carry bag, which works fine unless you already wear a daypack like I do. One solution is Double Bull's Wild Thing blind pack. It will hold your blind and other accessories on your back, where the weight carries much easier.

QUICK TIPS

- Get a comfortable chair with a backrest. A stool might be okay if you're 20 years old, but for the rest of us a nice back rest is the way to go. I typically fold my chair up when a shot is imminent, provided I'm paying attention and have the time.

- A bow holder of some kind is very handy. If your bow doesn't have parallel limbs, you may be able to use a wire bowholder that pushes into the ground. Otherwise, there are devices that attach to your stabilizer hole and create a tripod using your bottom cam as the back leg. The Vibracheck Quickstand is one such product.

- Devise a way to hang your pack from the hub structure of the blind, so the weight holds it down and prevents it from moving in strong winds.

- When hunting whitetails, use a fixed-blade broadhead (or some mechanicals, such as the Trophy Ridge Undertaker) and shoot through the see-through netting you've stretched across the shooting holes. Hung properly netting won't affect your point-of-impact, but will avoid spooking deer that don't like the black holes.

- Carry a soft, cushiony pad you can kneel on when it comes time to shoot. Also, practice shooting from your knees and from a chair, just in case you don't have time to eject to the ground. And always turn your chair to the right of your shooting hole if you're right-handed (opposite for lefties) so you can shoot from a natural position.

- Arrange your shooting holes to cover a wide swath in front of you, but make sure you have small, slit-like viewing holes to the sides and behind you. Surprises are a bad thing, so make sure you see them first.

- Don't overdo the shooting hole arrangement. Sunlight is your enemy, because it will light you up, making you susceptible to getting spotted. The darker the better.

- Wear all black clothing in a pop-up blind so you blend with the darkness. Black gloves, headnet, and top are essential to going undetected. A good blind will have black inside walls to contribute to the darkness.

- When hunting pronghorns in hot weather, make sure you bring plenty of water along to stay hydrated. It can get extremely warm in an enclosed blind. Some blinds have zippered roof panels and opening them, even just a crack, lets a lot of heat escape.

- Wear ultra-quiet clothing in a blind. You'll be dealing with very close ranges, and the swish of a noisy jacket will clear the area quickly.

- Take a kid along with you in the blind. Youngsters can sit on the ground or in a small chair and eat, drink, play with toys and fidget like most kids without spooking game. When the critters get close, the kids can settle down and watch the show. It's the perfect way to get kids involved.

- A good pop-up blind can be deadly when stationed near an elk wallow. Just keep the wind in mind, do a little cow-calling throughout the day, and be ready for action.

- When hunting pronghorns, make sure you stake the blind down so a gust of wind doesn't leave you sitting in your chair, in the wide open, looking stupid. It usually isn't necessary to cover the shooting holes, but stay back from them so you aren't spotted.

One thing I've found that works well is a lightweight pull-type golf cart. You can strap your blind to the cart, along with your turkey decoys, chairs, and even your bow, and pull the whole works to your hunting area. Of course, that only works in appropriate terrain where the brush isn't too thick or the ground too steep. A deer cart works well too and will hold more gear like multiple deer decoys.

Ground blinds allow you to hunt places you might otherwise neglect. In the Great Plains states, trees can be scarce while deer, antelope, and turkeys are plentiful. A ground blind set up in a field of large, round hay bales works exceptionally well. I've also had success tucking them into the

I tucked this blind into some red willows in South Dakota and hunted until dark. The next morning I returned before daylight and it was all gone. Someone drove through water up to the blind and stole everything! Don't leave your blind where it can disappear.

edge of large cattail swamps. And, though it's hard to believe, I have set up in a bare, wide-open alfalfa field and had antelope, turkeys, and even deer walk right past the blind. Add a decoy of some kind to any situation and you have a very deadly setup.

Be careful about leaving your ground blind out overnight. I once left a Double Bull blind, two deer decoys, two chairs (one for a cameraman), and a really nice deer cart in a large, wide-open wetland in South Dakota. When my cameraman and I returned in the morning darkness, it was all gone. Even the half bottle of water I'd left on the ground inside the blind was gone! Dirty thieves!

If you haven't hunted out of a ground blind, you're missing out on an "up close and personal" hunting experience.

CHAPTER THIRTEEN

Clothing is gear, and the right clothing helped me take this nice Alberta mule deer. It was a four-hour stalk, three and one-half hours on my belly, in the rain!

Clothing the Bowhunter

I didn't have a clue I'd been bellycrawling for well over three hours. I guess time flies when you're having fun.

Half expecting to see him gone, I slowly turned my head to make sure my cameraman was still in the grass behind me. He was still there, rain dripping off the brim of his rainsuit hood, camera safely tucked in a waterproof cover. Troy was only 24 years old, and I feel relatively certain he thought I was certifiably insane.

Seven mule deer bucks, two good ones, were bedded in the wet Alberta prairie grass less than 100 yards away. We'd been crawling on our bellies in 15-inch-tall grass for a long time. Occasionally, one of the bucks would stand to feed, halting our advance, then bed back down again. We had at least 50 yards to go with no cover besides the grass.

This isn't going to happen… I thought to myself, but being a clinically stubborn bowhunter, I wasn't giving up. I just hoped my cameraman would stick with me.

It was raining, not hard, but enough to make it miserable, when we started this stalk, which gives you a better idea of my mental state. That's also why we were wearing rainsuits from the start. The hunt was winding down, and I wanted a mule deer really bad. They've been my nemesis over the years, and I was determined to make this work regardless of weather.

By suspending our bodies on our elbows and tip-toes, we slinked along like inch-worms. I'd lay my bow out in front of me, then snake my way through thorny prairie rose bushes, repeating the process while keeping my head down.

Though I hadn't stood or sat up in three and a half hours, I remember feeling comfortable as I lay there in the spitting rain. Except for my hands, I was dry as a bone. I wasn't sweaty and clammy from perspiration, nor was I soaked from the rain.

My optimism grew with each inch we gained. *Maybe this will happen,* I thought. Then, as if on cue, all seven bucks stood and slowly fed away from us. None showed any inkling of suspicion, so I kept going. It paid off because the two largest bucks began to feed back toward us. A velvet-antlered buck was also giving us trouble, constantly looking around as if his only goal in life was to be a scout. He liked to lead the way and slipped ahead of the two bucks as they fed to our left. The velvet buck was only 40 yards away from a collision with our scent stream when I decided to slowly raise my head and range the second largest buck—53 yards.

I rolled over on my back and told Troy to get ready; I was going to take the shot.

To make a long story longer, I loaded my bow while lying on my back, sat up while drawing, and put my 50-yard pin a bit high on the closest buck. Only the velvet buck picked its head out of the grass to see the two of us pop up out of the ground like gophers. It was too late to warn his buddies, because my arrow was gone. The result was my best mule deer buck, a 30-incher that scored just over 170.

More importantly to me, it was the greatest stalk of my life. Jim, my guide, watched the four-hour stalk through his spotting scope from his dry truck a half-mile away. He also thought I needed one of those white jackets with really long sleeves!

The marketing slogan of one of my favorite hunting clothing manufacturers is: "Turning Clothing Into Gear." That couldn't be more true. Clothing is gear. That Alberta stalk was a perfect example. It's safe to say few hunters would have left their vehicle that morning, but because I was dressed for the job, not taking a run at those bucks wasn't an option. Your clothing can be a huge factor in your success. It can either enable, or limit, your hunting ability.

If you doubt clothing can make a difference, hunt with a cameraman who is wearing noisy clothing. It doesn't matter if it's the *swish-swish* of nylon pants when stalking or the rustling of windproof layers in a sweater while perched in a treestand. If your clothing is quiet, and their clothing isn't, it'll drive you insane. Okay, maybe that's just me.

After my complaining about the noisy clothing worn by one cameraman, he looked at me and said, "Curt, your standards are just too high." Though I suspect it was a criticism, I took it as a compliment.

When looking over hunting duds, the first thing I do is run my fingernail across the fabric. Then I scrunch it around between my fingers. If I get that far, I'll slip it on and move my arms around. It doesn't matter if the camo pattern is right, the fit is perfect, and the design functional, if that garment generates any noise, I look elsewhere.

That applies to outerwear. Let's start with undergarments first.

Rule number one — avoid cotton at all costs. It's fine around camp, or

High-tech compression fit undergarments look better on people like my New Mexico elk guide Pasqual Vallejos, than they do on me. The purpose of the tight fit is to spread the perspiration beads out so they evaporate faster.

Mossy Oak Apparel Vaportec and Under Armour Heat Gear.

Even in a sun-baked hide in Africa the right underwear is crucial for regulating body temperature. Say goodbye to the sweat-soaked, clammy feeling of cotton.

if you're hunting in a blazing hot antelope blind where wet clothing might feel good. Otherwise, cotton should be banned from your clothing arsenal. When it gets wet, either from perspiration or precipitation, it stays wet. Not only does that make you feel uncomfortable and clammy, it can contribute to hypothermia. Think about how long it takes for wet denim jeans to dry, and you'll get the picture.

From this day forward, increase your focus on the most important layer of clothing, the one next to your skin, often called the base layer. Perspiration is a fact of life for bowhunters, whether it comes from hiking into your treestand or climbing a mountain. Biologically, sweat is a good thing but only during exertion. After that, you must get rid of it by transporting it away from your skin. Today's high-tech fabrics do just that, and until you've tried them, you don't know what you're missing in the way of personal comfort. Companies like Under Armour, Sitka Gear, Mossy Oak Apparel, Medalist, and others manufacture undergarments with fabrics that do not absorb moisture but allow it to go to the next layer.

For example, I often wear Under Armour's Heat Gear next to my skin, with multiple layers over it. I'll still get that clammy feeling after working up a sweat hiking into my treestand, but within a half-hour or so I feel dry and comfortable, as if I just left the house. That never happened when wearing cotton underwear.

These thin, high-tech materials next to your skin also serve to reduce chafing when hiking, carrying backpacks, or riding horseback. The "slipperiness" allows your outer garments to move with your body, and when exerting yourself, you can actually feel the evaporation taking place. Once you splurge on yourself (these garments aren't cheap), you'll discover the comfort you've been missing.

Materials vary, as do thicknesses. When the temperature drops, you can opt for heavy or even expedition- weight base layers. Under Armour's Cold Gear is one option, and Cabela's MTP line is another.

In ultra-cold weather, consider the Body Sock from Carol Davis Sportswear. This one-piece high-performance undergarment is constructed of Polartec and Powerstretch, which makes it warm, comfy, and hydrophobic, so it wicks away moisture like the products mentioned above. I've worn my Body Sock on very cold days, and it's outstanding.

QUICK TIPS

- Tight "compression fit" undergarments like Under Armour are designed that way to spread out beads of perspiration so they evaporate quicker. It definitely works.

- If you're a traveling hunter, pay attention to the weight of the clothing you choose. Airlines are getting very restrictive on baggage weight, and heavy clothing adds up fast. Wool is outstanding, but it's very heavy, whereas fleece is warm and lightweight.

- Underwear tops with a turtleneck are warmer than those with a crew neck. They can chafe your neck if you're spending hours turning your head looking for game, but they will feel warmer and cover your neck.

- Don't just restrict your layering to your upper and lower body. Think about your feet. A pair of thin polypropylene socks will wick moisture away from your feet and provide a slippery layer to prevent blisters. Add layers of wool (not cotton) or synthetic socks as necessary. If it's really cold, slip a chemical toe warmer under your toes and your feet will never get cold again.

- I tend to avoid Velcro at all costs because of the noise. If a piece of hunting clothing has Velcro on I usually look elsewhere, or I'll remove the Velcro if it doesn't affect functionality.

- If it's too warm to wear any sort of gloves, then spread a little face paint on the back of your hands and fingers to camouflage their movement.
- If you do a lot of spot-and-stalk hunting, look for pants with reinforced knees and seats. The padded knees in King of the Mountain wool are priceless when stalking on your hands and knees or even when waiting for a bull elk to show up.
- Pants with lots of pockets will act like a fanny pack. Store some of your essentials in the pockets so they are where you need them as you get dressed each day.
- In hot weather, a bandana wrapped around your head will absorb sweat beads and keep them out of your eyes. It may also prevent your face paint from running.
- I like jackets with zippered pockets just for the security they provide. I can stuff my valuables, like releases and rangefinder, inside and know they'll stay there.
- Hoods on jackets are the work of the devil. I hate them and seldom wear any jacket with a hood unless it's a rainsuit. Hoods get in the way, blow in the wind, and when I have one on I feel like I can't see or hear like I should.
- On a bear hunt in Canada, or a September whitetail hunt, you might wish for a bug suit from Bug Tamer. The full, see-through hood alone is worth its weight in bear roasts.
- I find leather belts can squeak when worn underneath packs and certain types of clothing. For that reason I like to wear a belt made of other material like nylon web. Suspenders are another really comfortable option.
- 3-D leafy camouflage suits are favored by some bowhunters, but I admit to not having personal experience with this type of clothing. I'm sure they work fine, but I've always been concerned about getting hung up on brush or getting it caught in my bow.

I also have to mention natural undergarments. The soft Merino wool underwear made by Justin Charles is expensive, but it's extremely soft (doesn't itch), captures body heat, wicks moisture, and naturally suppresses odor. There's just something about wool, but we'll get to the outer garments in a bit.

Another great natural fabric is silk. Silk feels great on your skin (Did I say that?), doesn't absorb moisture, and dries very quickly. I wore black silk in Africa, and when the hide got oven-hot, I stripped down to just my black skivvies. Not only was I cool, but I disappeared in the dark blind. A huge zebra stallion never knew I was there!

Intermediate layers should also be synthetics such as Polartec, polar fleece, or Cabela's Micro-Tex, one of my favorite materials. Micro-Tex wears well, is comfortable, dries quickly, and above all, is quiet. Sitka Gear is another great product with the same qualities. Day One Camouflage also makes well-designed intermediate/outerwear constructed of super-soft fleece.

I tend to wear a shirt with a collar so binocular and rangefinder straps don't chafe my neck. I also like a breast pocket and pants with lots of pockets for gear I need quickly. I may be hunting in this layer, depending on the conditions, so I look for the camouflage pattern I want as well as quality material. If I get caught in a quick rain, or my legs get wet up to the knees from dew on the grass, I want clothing that will air-dry very quickly.

Once I'm fitted with undergarments and a pair of pants and shirt, I start looking at the thermometer to determine what layers I'll need under my outerwear. Of course, the type of hunting to be done is a huge factor. If you plan to spend the morning hiking up a mountain, you'll likely be strapping your next layer or two to your pack. This is one of the primary benefits of layering — adjusting quickly to exertion level and changing conditions. I always have an extra fleece in my pack, just in case.

A warm vest is a great piece of bowhunting gear because it will insulate your torso and kidney area but leave your arms and shoulders less encumbered with layers. That contributes to a smooth, easy draw and more natural shooting

Wool is still the best natural fiber for hunting, because it's quiet, repels light moisture, breathes, is still warm when it's wet, and the fabric doesn't reflect light like some synthetics. Besides, it just feels right.

motion, as opposed to being all layered up like the kid in the movie Christmas Story. I'm loving my Sitka Gear vest these days, because it's soft, quiet, warm, and lightweight.

Layers of fleece tend to work well for me. Fleece doesn't hold moisture, creates lots of insulating air space, dries fast, and is very lightweight. In cold weather I'll wear as much as two layers of fleece pullovers under my outer garment. I don't even care if they come in camouflage colors as long as I have an outer layer that's camo. Fleece pullovers are also quite easy on the hunting budget.

For some reason, I love to wear wool when hunting. It just feels good, but it's also functional. I have several wool outfits from King of the Mountain and Sleeping Indian, and they are well-designed and custom-fit. Wool is what I call "Caveman Gore-Tex" because if it has an open weave, like those mentioned, it allows body moisture to escape but still retains body heat. And, as you've read for years, wool is about the only material that retains its insulating qualities when wet. If I wear some high-tech undergarments under my wool, I am surprisingly comfortable, even on a warm day on a high country elk hunt or in the dank atmosphere of a caribou hunt.

Raingear is simply insurance against a lost day hunting. Heavy rain will keep you in camp, but light rain can make for some outstanding hunting because game can be active.

You can also get a denser weave in your wool to help ward off the wind in a treestand. Gray Wolf Woolens is one company that makes such a wool product, and I've worn their stuff as well. It's excellent.

On the negative side, wool is expensive, dries slowly, is heavy, and may require special cleaning procedures. I have machine washed my King of the Mountain and had no problems with shrinkage. One thing you won't do with quality wool is wear it out. A good wool outfit will last you for years, maybe a lifetime.

RAIN GEAR

Before we venture into really cold weather, let's address rain gear. The object here, of course, is to stay dry. Much depends on the type of hunting you'll be doing and what you expect from your rain gear.

If you're only concerned about staying dry in your treestand, you can get by with lesser rain gear. Rather than suffer through a long-term downpour, you'll likely be heading back to your vehicle anyway, especially if there's lightning. Slow drizzles can be warded off with economical rain gear that's packable enough to fit in your daypack. In such situations I wouldn't invest a lot of money in rain gear and may even stick with a camouflage poncho I could quickly throw over me until the rain stops.

If you hunt on the ground, it's a whole different story. Caribou hunters don't usually run into a lot of rain in September, but it is possible. They're also spending a lot of time in boats, often on rough water. A quality rainsuit with a layer of Gore-Tex, like those available from Cabela's or Redhead, will keep you dry in all but the most severe downpours. That said, if you're willing to spend serious cash on do-it-all rain gear, read on.

Elk hunters may opt for a high-quality rainsuit that's very light and compresses into a small space in their pack. Though rare, persistent heavy rain can occur, and you definitely don't want to get wet miles from camp. One option is Cabela's Space Rain Ultra packable rainwear, which is extremely lightweight and compresses nicely. I've also been known to carry a poncho in these situations too, because I can hunker down and wait for a break in the weather. Typically, high country rains are short-lived.

Now, if you're hunting the Pacific Northwest or coastal Alaska – all bets are off! Experienced bowhunters in these regions must endure long persistent downpours and usually laugh at any rain gear with a "breathable" membrane. Could you get by on a six-day hunt with average rain gear? Maybe, but are you willing to bet on it?

For these kinds of conditions I recommend serious rain gear designed solely for keeping you dry. Some of this stuff doesn't breathe like Gore-Tex, but it won't fail you when the going is very wet. This list includes the Downpour Series from Sitka Gear (somewhat breatheable and features a ventilation zipper), Rivers West's Back Country outfit (not breathable but has zipper vents), and Helly Hansen IMPERTECH, a popular option in Alaska that's soft, quiet, and waterproof but not breatheable and isn't available in camouflage at this writing. Just remember, the more waterproof a rainsuit is, the less it will breathe. You may have to adjust your activity level until the monsoon quits.

ULTRA-COLD

If it's really cold we'll have to add yet another layer of armor against the elements – as long as it isn't a noisy layer. The only exception is if there's a strong wind, where I need a windproof layer. Such layers are always noisier than I'm willing to tolerate, but the sound of the wind should muffle garment noise. This last layer of armor must have as silent an outer surface as practical for the conditions.

Once past the outer surface, consider the insulation you'll need. I generally avoid thick, bulky insulated jackets and coveralls, if possible. Layering still shines here, because you can just keep adding layers. Still, fleece doesn't resist wind well, so you may need to pull on a heavy pair of bibs and a jacket. Those with Thinsulate Insulation get the job done, and if it's really cold and windy, check out Arctic Shield's clothing, which is designed to reflect your body heat back at you.

It's easy to disappear in a winter landscape if you're wearing white or snow camo. The tough part is staying warm and still.

Sometimes, though, you just have to use common sense. Years ago, when I was young and dumb (or maybe just dumber), I hunted one morning so cold that my eyelashes froze to my binoculars. It was -22 F, and windy, as I glassed whitetails coming to bed in a large willow swamp. Those deer avoided my ground blind, leaving me kneeling in the snow and feeling stupid. I eventually came to my senses and headed home to watch football. I never should have crawled out of bed that morning. That was neither sane nor safe.

Regardless of weather, you'll have another consideration in your outer garments — the camouflage pattern. These days, there's no excuse for wearing outer garments that don't blend with the terrain you'll be hunting. The choices boggle the mind. In

The right gloves will hide your shiny hands and keep them warm. These Under Armour gloves even have fleece "snot wipers" sewn into the thumb and forefinger. Somebody was thinking!

the West you'll want a more open pattern to avoid looking like a black bear from a distance. Realtree Max 1, Mossy Oak Brush, and ASAT are excellent for western hunting.

Other patterns with lots of contrast like Realtree AP, Mossy Oak's Treestand and Mathew's Lost Camo will work in all kinds of terrain, and darker patterns like Mossy Oak Break-Up work when leaning up against dark trees or hunting the shadows or ground blinds. If you'll be hunting in a dark pop-up ground blind, wear black.

Will you be able to kill game wearing your old green plaid wool jacket? Well, yeah, but what fun is that?

Keeping your hands warm is crucial and easy. Thick, heavily insulated gloves just don't work for bowhunters, so we have to layer there as well.

On early season hunts when the weather is warm, wear a pair of thin, moisture-

QUICK TIPS

- When choosing rain gear, consider whether the outer fabric will hold moisture. You may be dry inside, but if the outer shell is soaked, it may stay wet for a long time. That's not a problem at home but it is when you're trying to find a place to store a wet rainsuit in a tent.

- Cheap, super lightweight rainsuits may keep you dry during a downpour when you're standing still weathering the storm, but they may not hold up if you're busting through alders or bellycrawling on a pronghorn. Don't expect too much from cheap gear.

- Don't concern yourself too much with the noise a rainsuit makes. Quieter is always better, but when it's actually raining most rainsuits are quiet enough because they're wet and the noise of the rain will cover you to some degree.

- I've yet to find thin, lightweight gloves that are waterproof for more than a few seconds. There are just too many seams. This is why you'll find a pair of gloves on my hands, another pair in my pocket and probably one or two more pairs deep in my pack.

- A hat with a brim that goes all the way around your head is great when elk hunting. It keeps the pine needles from funneling down your neck as you duck under pine boughs.

- Some bowhunters like to wear gaiters on their legs. In some conditions, especially when the grass is wet or there's a foot of snow on the ground, gaiters can be very beneficial for keeping your legs and feet warm and sealing moisture out of your boots. Certain types can be noisy, however.

- Pullover jackets and fleece tops are nice, but you lose the ability to zip them completely open when trying to regulate your body temperature on hikes.
- No camouflage pattern is more effective than snow camo. Tuck yourself into the snow-covered woods and you'll virtually disappear. It is also very effective in treestands against an overcast sky.
- If it's ultra cold and you don't have a hand muff, just put your chemical handwarmers in the pockets of your parka and keep your hands inside until it's time to shoot.
- Insulated bibs tend to be a better choice than coveralls. That's because you'll need the freedom of movement when climbing trees with lots of clothes on. Coveralls are warm but tend to restrict your arm movement.

wicking gloves. I really like Under Armour's gloves, which even have fleece snot-wipers sewn on the forefinger and thumb. Not only will such gloves keep your hands warm on cool mornings, but they'll cover those shiny hands, which are always moving.

As it gets cooler you can add another glove over your thin layer. Those green wool military surplus gloves are quiet, warm, and very inexpensive. Keep in mind, most insulated gloves are not only bulky but they tend to have waterproof linings, which are always noisy. To combat wet weather, I tend to carry several pairs in my pack and change them as they become wet.

In ultra-cold weather, the best gloves I've found are the Ragg wool gloves with Thinsulate Insulation. They are very warm and quiet but a bit bulky, so be sure to practice shooting with them on because they will change the way you grip your bow and your release.

I'm not much of a mitten guy, but some of the mittens with break-away finger sections do work well, as long as they don't have Velcro closures. Magnets are better.

The best solution for really cold weather is a hand muff that straps around your waist. Wear thin gloves to maintain dexterity and keep them in the muff for warmth. If it's below zero, just stuff a chemical handwarmer in the muff and you'll have toasty fingers. Be aware

Twenty-five percent of your body heat escapes from your head. I like a cap with a brim to keep the low sun out of my eyes, then a fleece balaclava with a long neck. If it gets really cold, I just add a knit facemask.

though, if you keep your hands too warm and have to grab a cold bow and hold it for long minutes with sweaty hands, you'll get cold fingers very quickly.

Because your noggin is the body's radiator, you must learn to regulate its release of body heat. When exerting myself on a long hike, or even when wearing too much clothing on my way to a stand, I take my hat off and leave it in my pocket or pack until I've completely cooled down. That allows my body heat to escape through my scalp and cuts down on perspiration elsewhere.

At the other end of the spectrum is *preventing* heat loss through your head, where 25 percent of your body heat gets away. If your head is warm, your body can devote more blood to your extremities. Neglect your head, and you'll be heading back to camp for hot coffee.

Since I spend a lot of time facing into a rising or setting sun, I always wear a hat with a brim of some kind to shade my eyes. In warm weather that means a ball cap I may turn around if I'm on my belly trying to look through grass. Or I may take it off too, especially in really windy conditions. The last thing I need when sneaking to the edge of a gully on a bed-

One very effective answer to cold weather is the Heater Body Suit. This sleeping-bag-like outfit goes over your regular hunting clothes and captures body heat. It's great in ultra-cold weather. Even in cool weather you can wear less layers on your body so you don't get sweated up going in.

ded pronghorn is to have my hat blow off and into the air.

When it gets cold I add a fleece pullover facemask or balaclava, but I put it over my cap with the brim sticking out. The brim also helps me cover my eyes in the presence of cautious whitetails. I don't like to make eye contact.

That combination keeps me warm until the frigid weather shows up in December. Then I simply add a knit facemask underneath the fleece for two full layers of insulation. If that doesn't keep my head warm, I go home.

The final solution for cold weather is a Heater Body Suit. This sleeping-bag-like garment is heavily insulated and covers your entire body except your head. Once on stand, you slip into the Heater Body Suit with a harness that goes over your shoulders. That holds the suit up when it's time to emerge for a shot. The Heater Body Suit contains your body heat and also conceals the movements of your arms and legs. When a shot presents itself, simply zip it open, slip out, and grab your bow. The suit will stay on your back, out of your way, and it is surprisingly quiet.

I've only scratched the surface of the clothing options available to the modern bowhunter. You may find combinations and materials that work better for you. I can only pass on what I've learned over 27 years of bowhunting experience.

If you treat your hunting clothing like gear and prepare for the unpredictable, it'll be much easier to hunt like there's no tomorrow.

CHAPTER FOURTEEN

Nothing happens if your boots don't allow it. If the fit is wrong, or you haven't broken them or your feet in, you'll be miserable. If the boots are right, you'll feel invincible.

Bowhunting Boots

"It's awfully steep here, so make sure you bring boots that are one size too big," advised my Montana elk guide in the summer of 2005. "If your boots are too small, you'll have a black toenail on your big toe by the time I get done with you."

He wasn't lying. The mountainsides we had to negotiate in the northwestern part of the state were nearly vertical. In some places, latching onto young pine trees when going downhill was the only thing preventing a freefall. I came through that hunt with my toenails intact, but I did spend considerable time stopping to adjust my socks and re-tie my boots!

That's just an example of the value of appropriate footwear and why this subject demands its own chapter.

The right boots can be elusive. It all depends on the game being hunted, the terrain, weather, and the time of year. The perfect all-around bowhunting boot doesn't exist, but there are boots perfect for specific types of hunting. We can't cover every scenario, but here are some thoughts.

With the high-quality linings sewed into today's supremely engineered boots, it's easy to think you don't have to break in a new pair before a hunt. That's wrong. It is possible to find boots that fit perfectly and wear well right from day one. I've had boots that required no break-in period. The problem is, you won't know if your chosen boots will fall into that category until you wear them. Don't assume anything.

I like to put on a new pair of boots and start off hiking with them on my treadmill. That way, if a hot spot develops I don't have to walk a long way home, making it worse. Once I've got a few miles on a pair of boots, and they feel good, I'll strap on a pack frame with 40 pounds of sand so I know how the boots feel with weight on my back. Breaking in new boots is much less of a project than it was two decades ago, but it still must be done.

Turkey hunters generally don't need warm boots since they're hunting in the spring, but in the Dakotas, for example, you could run into snow during a spring hunt. In the South, turkey hunters may be concerned about slithering reptiles and need snake-proof boots. Other areas will often require knee-high waterproof boots, because of the need to cross creeks and wet areas. And most turkey hunters end up doing quite a bit of hiking, so a pair of sloppy-fitting rubber boots can be disaster. Nothing wears through layers of skin like a pair of ill-fitting rubber boots.

For early fall spot-and-stalk hunts you may be able to get by with a boot that's ultra-light and un-insulated. Whenever I'm stalking game, I prefer a boot with the smallest footprint possible. That means a form-fitting sole rather than those heavy soles that extend outside the shape of your foot.

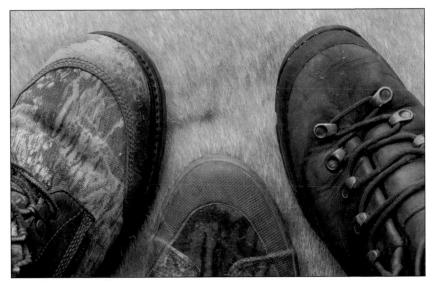

The boot on the left has a heavy, wide sole that is good for support. However, that extra 3/8" rim, on a pair of size 12 boots, computes to a total footprint about 15 sq. in. larger than boots without the rim.

Let's do a quick calculation. One of my size 12 boots measures 30 inches around the perimeter of the sole. The sole, a popular heavy-lugged design, extends three-eighths inch outside the edges of the leather upper, or profile of my foot. The total surface area of that portion of the sole is seven and one-half square inches – per foot. That's a total footprint 15 square inches larger than a sole that mimics the shape of my foot.

No matter the terrain, when I'm stalking game I don't want any larger footprint than necessary, because it increases the potential for game-spooking noise. That extra "lip" is especially troublesome when stepping over obstacles, as it can catch twigs, branches, and rock edges as I walk. A single such mistake can blow a half-day stalk.

If the stalk is very intense, in relatively easy terrain, I like the super-light canvas stalking shoes that look similar to high-top tennis shoes. On an Arizona elk hunt, I wore Cabela's Stalking Shoes and was able to slip through the cedars so quietly I couldn't even hear myself. Well, okay, maybe I could, but they were extremely silent. So quiet was I that I actually stalked too well, getting closer than I should have to a monster bull elk. The bull, an easy 400-class contender, ended up walking down the trail on which I stood and I was pinned down. When the massive beast got to five yards, he spotted me through a cedar tree and exploded into flight. I still get a twitch when I think of that encounter.

I also wore those shoes when hunting in hides in South Africa and Namibia. Plains game animals are extremely nervous, and the slightest sound can clear a waterhole in the blink of an eye. I know it sounds strange, but I actually had to stalk from one end of my blind to the other to turn on the camcorder and grab my bow. My quiet, lightweight shoes were much quieter than a bulky boot would have been. And much cooler, too!

I wore L.L. Bean Maine Hunting Shoes for many years while bowhunting elk and found the boots to be excellent. They gave me a small, silent footprint and kept the morning dew off my feet. They are a bit hot in an antelope blind, but in the right weather they work great. There are lots of other boots available with a minimum footprint that will serve you well when stalking. Danner Pronghorns have worked well for me, and boots by Lowa, Meindl, and Wolverine also come to mind.

Waterproof linings, such as Gore-Tex, can be invaluable in a boot. Wet feet will send you back to camp and may accelerate blistering. Be wary of cheap, imitation waterproof linings, as some will be very noisy when stalking. I also avoid the aggressive lugged soles on my stalking boots, because they tend to snap twigs and make crunching noises without warning. You need a boot that gives you some degree of "feel" in the sole. Be fussy, because an entire hunt may depend on a single stalk.

In some types of terrain, and on some hunts, you may need a heavy, wide sole for support and to protect your foot. That's especially true in rocky terrain where you could get your foot jammed between rocks or lose your balance and have to catch yourself in jagged boulders. Sheep or goat hunts would be examples, though I've not enjoyed one of those hunts yet.

However, on a caribou hunt in the Northwest Territories, I opted for a heavy soled boot with outstanding ankle support. Cabela's Mountain Hunters helped my feet withstand the constant transition from soft lichen to granite rocks, and even

Certain situations require a specific boot. When packing meat down a mountain you'll need boots with a strong sole and excellent ankle support.

though I have rubber ankles, there was no way I could have sprained an ankle in those boots. The lichen and rocks were very quiet to stalk on, so I didn't really give up anything either.

On moose hunts, especially in Alaska, you may need to cross creeks and streams. Some wear hip boots, but they can be difficult to hunt in and hard on your feet. Another option is the packable waders that slip over your boots. They're designed only for crossing streams but can save you from wet feet or having to hike miles to avoid a crossing. One company that offers such a product is Wiggy's, Inc.

When elk hunting, I may be wearing a lighter stalking boot, but you can bet I have a good pair of Danners, Wolverines, or similar well-built boots back in camp. When it comes to strapping 80 pounds of elk on my back, the last thing I need is wimpy boots with soft ankle support. You may think you're a tough guy in great shape, but all it takes is one misstep and you're on crutches for weeks.

QUICK TIPS

- When buying boots for turkey hunting, make sure the sole doesn't have any brightly-colored inlays that might catch the eye of a turkey as you sit on the ground.
- When in doubt, go with at least a half-size bigger on your boots. That allows for multiple pairs of socks and will keep your big toe from bottoming out on steep terrain.
- In most cases, you're better off removing the insole from your boots and installing a custom insole or an after-market one with extra support and gel for cushion and comfort. Any shoe store will carry a variety of cut-to-fit insoles with arch support. Pick one that feels good under your feet. To make room for your insole, you may need a half-size bigger boot.
- Always wear two pairs of socks when involved in serious hiking. This allows the two layers to move against each other, which is far better than having layers of your skin doing that. A pair of thin polypropylene socks under a quality wool sock works well in most situations.
- Carry some duct tape in your pack. If you start to feel layer separation on your feet, stop immediately and place some tape over the hot spot and put your socks back on. Moleskin and other kinds of tape will work too but aren't as legendary as duct tape!
- When attempting to walk quietly, always put your heel down and slowly roll down on the outside edge of your foot, taking care not to put your full weight down until it feels clear. You'd be surprised how many hunters don't

know how to walk in the stalking mode.

- On spot-and-stalk hunts, carry a pair of Baer's Feet or similar product. Typically constructed of fleece, these boot covers are designed to muffle noises as you stalk. They're also useful for quieting your footwork on a treestand and will even add warmth. Day One Camouflage also carries such a product.
- When the stalking gets really intense, don't be afraid to remove your boots and go those last few yards in your stocking feet. It's the ultimate in stalking silence, as long as your feet can take it.
- If you need a knee-high boot for a hunt that requires lots of hiking, like a moose hunt for example, make sure you get an ankle-fit boot that won't flop around and generate blisters. You'll definitely need to break-in this type of boot, and your feet, before your hunt. This also goes for hip boots when needed.
- Many Canadian guides and hunters favor knee-high rubber boots with removable liners that can be pulled and dried out. They're inexpensive and work very well in the bush, but they don't offer much ankle or arch support. They're made by Kamik.
- Some ankle-fit boots may trouble those with a high arch when putting them on and taking them off. Look for rubber boots with side zippers to alleviate this problem.
- When choosing any boots for treestand hunting, make sure they have a good heel built into the sole. A heel makes it much safer when climbing tree steps or ladders.
- Buy cold-weather boots a size larger than usual, not only to allow room for socks, but because tight-fitting boots restrict blood flow to your toes.
- In cold weather, it's crucial to dry the inside of your boots each day. Invest in a Peet boot dryer and use it every night. I also have a portable dryer that goes with me on cold weather hunting trips. If you don't have access to a boot dryer, crumpled up newspaper stuffed into your boots at night will help pull moisture out.
- In ultra-cold weather, keep a supply of chemical toe-warmers (these require less oxygen and are more efficient inside a boot than a hand warmer) with the adhesive backing on them. Stick one to each sock, under your toes, and you won't be leaving your treestand because of cold feet. If con-

siderable walking is necessary, put the warmers over your toes.

- When standing on a metal treestand platform, cover it with a thick kitchen rug or pad of some kind to insulate your feet from the cold metal.

- Try spraying your feet with a scent-free anti-perspirant before putting your first layer of socks on. It may inhibit sweating and keep your feet drier and thus warmer.

- For the ultimate cold-weather foot protection, get a pair of insulated "over-boots." Boot Insulators by Arctic Shield and Boot Blankets by Icebreaker Products, work well.

Whitetail hunters will have different needs for footwear. Most of us like to wear knee-high rubber boots to cut down on the scent we leave in the woods. It's hard to say just how much rubber boots prevent that, but they certainly don't hurt, and it's easy to see they would be better than leather boots. A product called Elimitrax is an over-boot system with a scent-free sole that helps to eliminate the problem of having a doe pick up your trail with her nose.

Waterproof knee-high boots are also necessary in wet con-

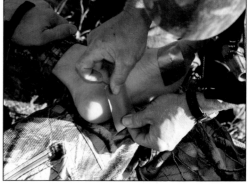

Even if you have good boots and two layers of socks, you can still get layer separation on your feet. Carry some duct tape and cover the hot spots before they become blisters.

ditions or anytime you're hunting near creeks or swamps. Rubber boots, built by companies such as LaCrosse, Muck, Rocky, and others, come in various designs and camouflage patterns, but it's their insulating properties that are most important. Un-insulated boots are fine for early season, but it doesn't take much of a drop in temperature to give you cold feet. I have several pairs of knee-high boots with various amounts of Thinsulate Insulation ranging from 200 to 600 and even 1,000 gram.

When things get nippy, it may be time to upgrade to a heavier boot with 1,000 gram insulation or even more. It depends on the exertion level of your hunt. If you're hiking snow-covered mountains for late-season mule deer or goats or even cold-weather caribou, you'll want a warm boot with an aggressive sole that has lots of support and grip. Traction and warmth become more important than stealth in those conditions. There are lots of options for every budget, just make

Who knows whether or not knee-high rubber boots help contain your scent, but there's no sense tempting fate. When whitetail hunting, always wear some kind of high boot.

sure it's a well-built boot with a waterproof/breathable lining and plenty of ankle support.

Once the weather turns really cold and there's snow on the ground, it probably means you're doing some late-season stand or blind hunting for whitetails. Under these conditions, I don't mess around with average footwear. I go straight to my pac-style boots with wool liners, or some of the high-tech boots like Cabela's Inferno Pac Boot. Mine have 2,000 gram Thinsulate Ultra and do a good job of keeping my feet warm in the worst conditions.

Even with the warmest boots, I still use chemical toe-warmers in ultra-cold weather. I stick one under my toes on each foot and slip my feet into my boots. Since I've been doing that, cold feet are but a memory. My feet are my weakness. I must keep them warm or I'm done hunting.

That's really the point of this chapter. You can have a sore shoulder or a headache, but if your feet are hurting, you're done. This is not the place to save a buck. Take care of your feet or pay a far higher price.

When a mature whitetail buck curls his lip to vacuum air, you'd better hope you were paying attention to the wind and your scent stream.

Scent Management

He knew something was wrong, and I expected it.

The bull elk stood statue-still, huge brown eyes scanning the timber for something he expected to see – another elk. I'd been squealing like a love-sick cow, and he desperately wanted to meet her.

I was tucked into the cover of three small pines, my release clipped on the loop and my arrow quivering on the rest. The knuckles on my bow hand were getting white and my temples throbbed. It was one of those moments an elk hunter lives for. Then it all changed with one step.

The bull took a cautious step to his left, and I knew, though it was just a small step, that this encounter was over. The bull's caution was ignited by his failure to see the cow. His only recourse was to see if he could locate her with his nose. Sadly, what he located didn't smell anything like an estrus cow. It smelled like me. A human. And a particularly stinky human at that!

In bowhunting, there's no more helpless feeling than watching a suspicious animal walk toward your scent stream. That's especially true when hunting elk, because it's difficult, if not impossible, to control your scent with so much physical exertion involved and a shower typically days away.

Still, there are ways we can manage the two types of scent we're concerned with, human and lure/cover scents. Let's start with human odor.

MANAGING OUR SCENT

I don't believe it's possible to eliminate human scent. There, I said it.

It just can't be done under practical hunting conditions, maybe not even under laboratory conditions. At least not well enough to completely fool a whitetail, elk, or the family dog.

The olfactory sense is different from other senses. The detection of odor is ultra-quick because of a biological "shortcut" to the brain in mammals. There's no hesitation or delay, no thinking, just reaction when a game animal smells danger. The same goes for us. Rub the beams of that bull elk you killed a few years back and smell your hands. You'll instantly recognize the odor and be transported to the high country in a flash.

It's no secret. The single best way to manage human scent is to use the wind. Trouble is, that isn't always possible, because we have no control over wind direction and variability, or the location and travel patterns of the game we hunt. Even so, the best bowhunters are always conscious of the wind. In the big city, far from any hunt, I even find myself noticing changes in wind direction and velocity. It's become a habit.

If you have any hope of using the wind, you must be able to monitor it, and that means having some type of wind indicator close at hand. Many options come to mind, and I often use several at once. The first thing I do is tie a length of dental floss or similar material to the end of the stabilizer on my bow. It's not much help in the rain, but otherwise it helps me constantly monitor wind direction, whether I'm in a tree or on the ground.

My favorite is a puff bottle, which works in any weather. Yes, it requires some hand movement to extract from a pocket and operate, but the cloud of talc, ashes, whatever, is super-sensitive to wind direction and will help you understand subtle changes in direction as the cloud rides the breeze. That's important in mountainous terrain or even when in a treestand in hilly country. The wind can do strange things and even make a promising stand location worthless because of the way the wind reacts to the terrain.

When hunting on the ground, I always keep my puff bottle in an easy-to-reach pocket, and I use it constantly, especially when the wind is light or the terrain undulating. Wind tends to funnel up or down draws and rivers or creeks; and thermals, while typically down in early morning, up in late morning, and down in the evening, can be unpredictable in some situations. The wind is a very untrustworthy friend.

QUICK TIPS

- Another good wind indicator can be made from weed seeds or tufts of fluff that can be pulled from a handy container and allowed to ride the breeze.

- On major hunting trips, take at least two puff bottles along. If you aren't using them up, you aren't using them enough.

- On open prairie cut with brushy draws and coulees, the wind can be very unpredictable. Seldom does it blow perpendicular through a significant draw, and I've seen it turn 60 degrees or more just to flow up or down a draw, depending on the angle. Use this knowledge to decide whether to approach a draw from the high side or low.

- When hunting in mountainous terrain you can almost always count on the breeze flowing downhill the moment the sun sinks behind a mountain. The air cools very quickly and sinks. That can help you or hurt you, depending on whether you're paying attention.

- Hunting from a treestand doesn't protect you from the wind. Unless there's a strong breeze, your scent will settle to ground level in the evenings. It'll be doing the same thing in the very early morning, but as the sun rises, so does your scent as a rule. Keep that in mind when deciding whether to hunt in the morning.

- Today's Internet weather forecasts are amazingly accurate in predicting wind direction, even hour by hour. Find your favorite weather site and monitor the wind forecast.

It's essential that you have some method of monitoring the wind. A length of dental floss or some other lightweight material tied to your stabilizer works well. You'll also want a puff bottle or floaters to tell you what the wind is doing away from your location.

Knowing the wind direction is elementary but not always enough. Things happen. Game animals walk where they aren't supposed to walk. Forecasts are wrong and the wind changes direction and swirls at will. Who hasn't been burned by a change in wind direction?

To prepare for such scenarios we try to do the best we can to reduce our scent stream. Some hunters become almost obsessive/compulsive about their scent control. I don't get that carried away. However, my "scent theory" is this: Any measure taken to reduce human scent can't hurt.

I try to envision my scent stream as a visible toxic cloud spreading across the terrain like fog. As the odor grows in strength, the cloud becomes larger and more dense.

Now, imagine your quarry downwind. He's smelled humans before, and he knows they're trouble, but he doesn't explode at the tiniest hint of human scent. If he detects a rancher fixing fence a half-mile away, it's not cause for alarm. However, if the strength of that human scent exceeds a pre-determined alarm level, he's gone. No one knows how animals think but that's my theory.

Consequently, the goal is to keep that scent stream as narrow and weak as possible. Make that animal believe you are either a half-mile away or you were there yesterday, or last week. It's not easy, and often impractical, but you can do things to make it happen.

I've found, when whitetail hunting, if I take all the traditional measures to make myself as scent-free as possible, it helps significantly.

First, get your hunting clothes clean and scent-free by washing them in one of the various odor-eliminating detergents. Is one better than another? I don't know; I can't tell. All you can do is get your clothes clean and hang them up to dry, then store them in a scent-free container such as a rubber tub. Some hunters like to throw pine needles or cover-scent wafers in with their clothes, but I've always felt if I'm working to be scent-free, that applies to all scents. I don't want a deer noticing anything other than ambient odors.

Now, a word about carbon-lined clothing. Does it work? I don't know; I can't tell. It's sort of like the broadhead debate in that no real-world testing can be done. I do know bowhunters who swear by their carbon clothes and wouldn't hunt without them. I have used various carbon garments, and I do know if I go through the entire scent-control ritual laid out here, I do feel there is a benefit to using carbon. How much the carbon contributes to the cause is hard to quantify, but if something gives you confidence, then use it. Forget the wind? Well, no.

Whether or not rubber or carbon-lined, knee-high boots eliminate leaving a scent trail in the woods is up for debate. I've seen deer ignore my entrance trail many times while wearing rubber boots, but I've never seen a coyote or fox miss my trail. That tells you something. Do rubber boots leave less scent than leather? I think so.

Just prior to my hunt, I shower with scent-eliminating soaps and shampoos. There are many products on the market designed to kill bacteria and slow the formation of new bacteria, the primary source of odor. Fresh perspiration doesn't smell, but once bacteria starts to grow, so does your "toxicity." Again, there are countless related products too numerous to mention here. Find ones that appeal to you and use them religiously.

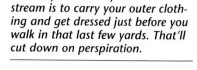

One way to reduce your scent stream is to carry your outer clothing and get dressed just before you walk in that last few yards. That'll cut down on perspiration.

Perspiration is your enemy now. Getting to your hunt location without getting all lathered up is your goal. If you have a lengthy hike ahead of you, wear just enough clothing to stay cool, then add appropriate layers a hundred yards or so before you get to your stand. Dressing at the base of your tree can leave too much scent around.

Once in the tree, pull out your favorite scent-killing spray and treat your outer clothing, including your hat, a major odor source. I spray mine inside and out, as well as my hair (make sure the product is safe for your skin). I also spray my pack.

If I do all those things, at the very least I feel confident I've done all I can to reduce my toxic cloud. And I've seen it work. I've had wily old does get downwind of me and stop what they were doing, raise their noses up and strain to vacuum in my scent. They'd look around, then dismiss the odor as not being at their alarm level (I assume) and go back to what they were doing. It doesn't always work that way, but maybe, just maybe, it will make the difference someday when a big buck raises his nose to your wind.

LURE SCENTS

Lure scents work. They can be a pain to use, but they do produce shot opportunities, and that's the bottom line.

Certain species of game are more susceptible to lure scents than others. I don't bother with scents for pronghorn antelope, mule deer, or moose, but they can enhance your elk hunting. Elk scents placed at a waterhole or wallow can lure a bull into range, and I've worn Cow Estrus Scent Wafers on my hat when still-hunt-

QUICK TIPS

- Don't store your hunting clothes in a plastic garbage bag, as it could contain some residual odor. They are a petroleum-based product.

- Human hair is often used as a deer repellent, so during the white-tail season, when your scent management is most critical, keep your hair as short as possible. Does it help? Well, it can't hurt.

- Carry a spray bottle of scent-eliminator and spray yourself before adding the last layer of clothing and then after, once you're in the tree or blind.

- If you're hunting something besides whitetails, spraying down with scent eliminator can be beneficial. Setting up an ambush at a waterhole or wallow for elk is one example.

- Do not spray scent-eliminator on the grip of your bow. It could be slippery when you prepare to take a shot.

- The effectiveness of clothing lined with carbon, silver fibers, anti-microbial treatments, and other technologies will always be up for debate, because it's so difficult to prove efficacy. Again, do they hurt you? No.

- Your breath is a major source of odor, so you may want to try some of the gums that promise to de-scent your mouth. Can't hurt.

- I don't recommend carbon-lined clothing for a hunt that involves lots of exertion. You may get by with some of the thinner garments, but thick carbon will trap body heat and you'll sweat like crazy on an elk hunt. The thicker, heavier carbon clothing also tends to be noisy.

- Maintaining scent-free entrance and exit trails can be accomplished with a product called Elimitrax, a hip-high over-boot with a scent-free sole. I've never seen a deer smell my trail when I wore Elimitrax, and I hear tell they're coming out with a knee-high boot.

ing and believe they helped cover my scent (more on that later) as well as stunk up my hat. A spritz of elk scent on a calling setup can also help your cause at times.

Most of your lure scent efforts, however, will be aimed at whitetails. In the early season, say September and early October, you're essentially appealing to a deer's curiosity. Once that deer is up and wandering around, it's got nothing better to do than investigate odd, appealing smells. Yes, they're working their way between feeding and bedding areas, but in early fall there is no urgency to find a mate or put on fat reserves for the winter. Giving them something to sniff and locate can be effective. What else do they have to do?

Various scents can lure a deer into bow range just by being left as a trail on the ground or even hung from a limb. They can be scents containing deer urine or other by-products, or they might be curiosity scents like anise oil, for example. Wildlife Research Center makes a scent called Trail's End #307 that smells a bit like licorice, but it contains a blend of natural ingredients that attract deer. It's hard to say why, but it does, as do other products that are not specifically "rut" scents.

From late October through December we concentrate on appealing to the noses of rut-focused bucks. Glandular scents such as tarsal and estrus lures come into play, and there are myriad products out there. Everyone has his or her favorites.

The real art of using lure scents revolves around how you dispense them. I'm a believer in using a drag rag when I have to walk through lots of deer habitat on my way to my stand. I'll soak up a felt drag, like the

If you have a long hike to your tree-stand, put some scent, either attractant or sexual, on a drag rag and leave a trail. I hang my drag in a tree about four feet up in my shooting lane.

Pro-Drag from Wildlife Research Center, with an appropriate scent, usually doe estrus, then tie the string to a stick so I can hold it out away from my own trail. I typically drag it to my stand site then wedge the stick into a branch so the drag hangs about four feet off the ground, in my shooting lane. It doesn't always work, of course, but it has pulled a buck into my ambush often enough that it's part of my arsenal.

Countless products will store and dispense your favorite scent. Felt wicks can be dipped into a scent bottle and hung from a branch, up off the ground, so it travels further, increasing effectiveness. Small canisters containing scent can be hung from branches, then retrieved and sealed when you leave.

Both Wildlife Research Center and Hunter's Specialties offer a full line of scents and dispensing products designed to get your scent into a buck's nose while keeping it off your hands and clothing. Experiment with various scents and dispensing techniques and you'll find one that gives you confidence.

COVER SCENTS

Cover scents are another enigma. Fred Bear once wrote about encountering a sow grizzly with her head buried in the body cavity of a dead, rotting horse. The wind swirled and the grizzly's head snapped out of the horse's putrid rib cage and looked directly in Fred's direction. If that grizzly could discern a whiff of human scent through the stench of that horse, it makes me wonder if we can fool an animal's nose at all!

Still, we're going to try, because we're stubborn that way. Defeating the olfactory system of every animal we hunt, save turkeys, becomes a challenge in itself. Drowning out our own scent with another can work. Fox urine, for example, can

QUICK TIPS

- A couple of cotton balls in a film canister will hold and dispense your scent, but since film is going away, look at some of the canisters available from various manufacturers.
- Wear latex examination gloves when using scents. They help keep the odor off you, your clothing, decoys, and vehicle.
- Ziploc bags can be your friend when dealing with scents. Even if you don't think you spilled any on the bottle, keep it in a tightly sealed Ziploc bag.
- To conserve scent, you can simply set the bottle on the ground with the cover off. Keep in mind, scent that's too strong can spook deer at times.
- Lure scents in gel form are popular because you can simply shove a small branch into the bottle and your scent will remain fresh and in place longer.
- A Scrape Dripper from Wildlife Research can be filled with lure scent and hung over a scrape. It's designed to drip only during daylight and can draw and hold a buck in the area.
- A Buck Bomb is an aerosol can that atomizes a scent and sends it deep into the woods for excellent coverage.
- Lure scents in solid form, like Wildlife Research's Trophy Leaf and Hunter's Specialties Scent Wafers, are very effective and mess-free. They can be hung on a branch or a hat and then returned to their container.

cover the scent trail we leave when walking in to our stand.

While hunting elk in Arizona a few years back, I attached a cow elk urine scent wafer to my cap as I stalked through the cedars. The wind was very unpredictable, and I felt I had to do anything I could to cover my odor. It seemed to work as I had elk around me that did not explode into flight. They smelled something but seemed confused by the odor. Of course, the bulls were desperate to believe a cow was near. The hesitation created by that confusion earned me a couple of shot opportunities on bulls I didn't want to take. Nevertheless, I can say with confidence their reaction would have been different had I not been using a strong cover scent.

Because cover scents are typically strong, they must be handled with care. Rubber or latex gloves and Ziploc bags are standard equipment when using these products.

Scent control as a whole is elusive, complex, and requires effort. Does it make you a more effective bowhunter? I don't think there's any doubt about it. Whether you're controlling your own scent or giving the game animals something to smell, you can tip the odds in your favor.

And, at the risk of sounding repetitious, you've got nothing to lose.

CHAPTER SIXTEEN

It was 1986 when this Minnesota buck taught me a lesson about calling big game. It took only two grunts to bring him on a string 300 yards across an open wetland.

Calling the Wild

It was one of those experiences, early in my bowhunting career, that stuck. Ten minutes that have lived in my memory banks for more than two decades and jump out at me every time I think about calling deer.

It was a heavy overcast morning, and I was perched in a lone cottonwood tree in the middle of a massive cattail and cane swamp in western Minnesota. The tree grew from the top of a small mound and fed off the minerals flowing from a tiny spring. I could see a mile in every direction.

Shortly after daylight, a really good white-racked buck emerged from a distant cornfield and headed for the security of the swamp. He was at least 300 yards away and not heading in my direction at all. I had to do something.

I pulled a call out of my pocket and sent a grunt toward the buck. Distance and the sound of his own walking prevented him from hearing the grunt, so I pumped up the volume for another grunt.

That time he heard it.

Without hesitation, the buck turned 90 degrees to his left and started walking directly at me. He didn't detour a foot for the entire 300 yards, knowing exactly where that grunt came from across the swamp.

I shook uncontrollably, especially after seeing the odd character of his rack and realizing he would make Pope and Young. As if he'd done it many times before, the buck walked right up on top of the mound so he, too, could survey the swamp. I zipped an arrow through his lungs from 22 yards and he collapsed in sight, 75 yards away.

I've imagined that same scenario many times, except with lots of trees between the buck and me, preventing me from knowing he was even there. That buck would have walked up to me even if I didn't know he was there – as long as I was calling at the right time. That's why I have confidence in "blind" calling.

Calling whitetails is sort of like fishing for muskies. When you cast big heavy

Your bag of tricks should contain at least one, or better yet two, grunt calls. You never know which sound will help you trigger a buck into detouring your way.

lures for hours on end, you're really hunting for a musky, but not just any musky. You're looking for that one fish that's in the right mood at the right time. Attempting to call a buck into bow range, regardless of the sounds used, is much the same. Not every buck will come running, or even walking, but sooner or later your call will reach the ears of the right buck on the right day. That's the payoff of your effort.

The options for deer calls are mind-boggling. Grunt calls come in all shapes and sizes. One of my favorites is the Primos Buck Roar, because it has the softest, most natural grunt I've found, and you can push a lot of air through it for an aggressive roar without it locking up. It also has a snort-wheeze call built into it for versatility.

Speaking of versatility, my other favorite call is the Hunter's Specialties True Talker. By varying the position of your finger, you can make just about any grunting sound a deer makes, and it is very dependable. Another good one is the Rack Blaster from Knight & Hale. It operates at both ends, either inhale or exhale, and comes with a retractable lanyard. There are others, of course, and you'll have to be the judge of what works for you.

Bleat calls have morphed into mostly can calls, the kind you tip over. These calls work well, because the action of the diaphragm inside gives the bleat a sort of natural-sounding quiver. Many a buck has lost his life responding to a can call, and Primos Hunting Calls got that ball rolling. Others are made by Hunter's Specialties and Knight & Hale. I keep one of these so-called "gravity calls" in my pocket at all times so it's handy. Quaker Boy has put their variation on these calls by adding a rubber squeeze bulb. The Squeezin' Bleat is operated by softly squeezing the bulb, and it has good tone.

"Jigging for bucks" involves using a heavy stick tied to the end of your pull-up rope. By jigging the stick up and down in the dry leaves you simulate chasing deer. On a calm morning that can bring a buck running!

A snort-wheeze can be made with your mouth but it sounds better and has more volume if you use a call with an air restrictor in it. Either way, just give out two short *ffftt – ffftt* sounds and a hard *fffffffffffffffffffffff* with lots of spit flying. This call will either goad a dominant buck into charging in or scare him and others off. I use it as a last resort when nothing else is working.

Rattling is another technique we all use from time to time. A good pair of fresh antlers sounds the best, but they can be a pain to carry around and use. Slamming a pair of antlers together up in a tree isn't very inconspicuous either. I'd rather use antlers but have mostly resorted to a rattling bag, which is a small bag filled with dowels of various shapes and materials. It slips easily into my pack, doesn't take up much room, and is silent when I'm not using it. Rolling it between your hands, creating the rattling sound, is much less obtrusive in a leafless tree in November.

Some bowhunters claim they get better results from real antlers, but I think we all give animals too much credit for thinking. If a buck can discern the difference between a rattling bag, a set of antlers, and a real fight from a distance, I'd be very impressed.

Finding the right buck is especially important when rattling. It doesn't work even a majority of the time, particularly in areas where the buck-to-doe ratio is

QUICK TIPS

- If you see a buck that's not coming your direction, don't wait to call to him. It's very difficult to make a buck turn around or come in a direction opposite of where he is headed. If you grunt or bleat to him before he gets past a point-of-no-return, you'll have better results.

- When blind calling big game, I use a passive approach first. With deer, I'll start with a soft bleat from a gravity call then work my way up to more aggressive calls. That way I don't spook a buck that may be close.

- When calling to a deer you can see, don't overdo it. Get his attention, and don't call when he's looking straight at you. If he turns to leave, call again.

- Typically, once a whitetail buck decides to ignore your calling, he's going to tune you out completely. However, try another call, switch from a grunt to a bleat, a can call or snort-wheeze, then rattle. Maybe a particular sound will trip his trigger. You seldom have anything to lose by trying.

- It's a good idea to carry two grunt calls in case one fails, freezes up, or you drop your call out of the tree.

- In very cold weather use a grunt call that is operated by inhaling. That will prevent it from freezing, because your warm breath doesn't get on the reed.

- If you do use real rattling antlers instead of a rattling bag, cut the brow tines off and the tips of the beams and upright tines. It'll be much easier on your hands and knuckles and safer if you fall on your antlers.

- An elastic bungee cord wrapped around your rattling antlers will keep them from rattling when you don't want them to.

- The best time to rattle is during the pre-rut, or mid-to-late

October in the upper Midwest. Once the chase phase gets going I don't have much luck with rattling as the bucks are concentrating on the does. You could have a different experience, so keep it in your arsenal.

- Avoid rattling in the late season. It doesn't seem to work on bucks, and it will clear the does out of your woods. The last thing a doe wants to see at that time of year is another aggressive buck.
- Make sure your pack contains grunt, bleat, snort-wheeze calls, and rattling antlers/bag at all times. You never know when you may have to plead with a monster buck to come your way, and you'll want to speak all the languages.

skewed toward too many does. However, before you start rattling, make sure your bow is loaded and handy, because a buck could come running.

To add authenticity to my rattling I like to do some grunting at the same time, and if I'm rattling for someone else and I'm on the ground, I'll kick up a fuss in the leaves and rake the ground and the trees to simulate a fight.

Another method of calling I've been experimenting with for several years now is what I call "jigging." I attach a heavy two-foot-long stick or dowel (even used my camera tripod in a pinch) to my pull-up rope and lower it to the ground from my treestand. On quiet days, when there are lots of dry leaves on the ground, I simply start bouncing it in the leaves like I'm jigging for fish. (One prototype looks like a police night stick with a cord attached to the tip of the handle. The one end hits the ground first, then the entire length of the main dowel, then the handle.) The thumping and the rustling leaves can get quite loud, and it sounds like there's chasing going on. I'm also grunting and bleating at the same time.

As far as I'm concerned, bowhunting elk is on a different plane. No other type of bowhunting comes close, and the sound of bugling bulls is a major part of the allure.

I've seen this tactic work quite well in attracting rutting bucks in quiet woods. They can't stand the thought of a buck chasing a doe, or even just a stray doe wandering around in the woods, and they come to investigate. That's when they spot my decoy(s) but that's for the next chapter.

Elk hunters live for calling. The sound of bugling bulls has coursed through my veins since the very first time I heard it in the wild. I was in Montana's Little Belt Mountains, and on the first morning of my hunt a bull answered my Larry D. Jones stainless steel reed call. I was pumped!

I also made every rookie mistake possible as I ran foward on a collision course with the bull. To make a long story short, the heavy-beamed 5x5 charged toward me, wide-eyed and snot flying, and I proceeded to shoot him square in the antlers! I called him back and missed him again at 25 yards when my arrow hit a stump. Never, after 23 years of hunting elk, have I run into a bull that was hotter than he was.

I was so shook up, just drawing my bow was a real challenge. I learned a lot from that bull, and he was the subject of the first article I ever sold to Bowhunter Magazine. The sound of his scream resonates in my soul to this day, and he's the reason I'll hunt elk until my legs can no longer carry me up the mountain.

I love to hunt any animal that can be called, but especially elk. Over the years, I've used lots of different elk calls, but I learned to use a diaphragm call and managed to get pretty good with one. It takes more practice than any call out there, but once you have it mastered you can make any elk sound you'll need.

Diaphragm calls come in many shapes, sizes, and designs. These days I like to use the calls from Primos that have the Sonic Dome. They require less volume of air and don't wear out as quickly as some other diaphragms. Their Sound Plate mouth calls have the same features to a degree, and I used them for many years as well. Other good ones are made by Wilderness Sound Productions, Quaker Boy,

This is just a small sampling of elk calls. Grunt tubes, cow calls, and mouth diaphragm calls should all be a part of your repertoire. Sometimes a cow call is all you need. Other times, a snot-blowing bugling match does the trick.

Hunter's Specialties, and Knight & Hale.

It will require patience and practice to learn how to call elk with a diaphragm, but you can't beat them for sound and versatility and particularly when making grunting and chuckling noises. Just remember, most bull elk couldn't win a bugling contest, and sounding like a young, reckless bull is usually more effective than acting like you're the biggest bull on the mountain.

Outside-the-mouth diaphragm calls are also very good and much easier to use. The Primos Terminator elk bugle is excellent, and they have a new one called the Baffle Bugle that I'm anxious to take to the mountains. Others include the H.S. Mac Daddy and the Power Bugle from E.L.K. Inc. the Quaker Boy Challenger Elk Bugle and Knight & Hale's Dead Bull Walkin'. Just a reminder, you are reading a book, so keep in mind the market is constantly changing and new calls are being invented and introduced all the time. Do your research, pick a call, and learn to use it. Of course, experience is your best, and most fun, teacher.

QUICK TIPS

- Some hunters can't use a diaphragm call because of an involuntary gag reflex. I've never had a problem, but make sure it doesn't bother you before committing to that style.

- On the other hand, I can't use the reed calls with the exposed reed. They tickle my lips and I can't get past it. Experiment with all types of calls until you find one you like.

- When using a diaphragm call, you must be careful it doesn't become lodged in your throat.

- If, like me, you keep your diaphragm call between your cheek and gum when not using it, you'll tend to feel like you're not thirsty. You are. Make every effort to take in plenty of fluids, or you'll get dehydrated.

- Like turkeys, elk can get fussy about the calls to which they'll respond. Carry several different styles of diaphragm calls, both inside and outside the mouth, and give the elk what they want.

- Don't call when an elk gets close. They are experts at pinpointing the exact location of a mew or bugle, and if they don't spot an elk, they may get suspicious and head downwind. Get them coming your way, then make them look for you.

- Don't set up to call near a ridgetop. A bull may come in and stop as soon as his head clears the horizon. He'll scan for other elk with only his head and neck exposed, and you won't have a shot.

Cow calls have become my first choice when I think elk are close. Should there be a skittish bull nearby and you just start blaring on your grunt tube, you could spook him off without ever knowing he's there. A couple soft cow calls are best for breaking the silence. A bull will often scream back to a cow call, and then you're in business. If I get no response after waiting and listening for a few minutes, I may graduate to a squeal.

Another entire book could be written about elk-calling techniques, but here we're trying to get you equipped with the calls you need. Most of my cow-calling is done with the diaphragm call that's already in my mouth. A diaphragm doesn't require me to use my hands, and I can call at full draw to stop a bull or even after the shot to shorten the bloodtrail.

That doesn't mean I only use diaphragm calls. I like squeeze calls like the Primos Hoochie Mama as well as the reed calls that look like a miniature trumpet. Good ones include the Primos Call Girl, Wayne Carlton Lonesome Cow call and Knight and Hale's Mountain Mistress.

OTHER SPECIES

When it comes to calling big game animals, I think the number one thing to remember is to give yourself options. Carry a number of different calls, and let the game tell you which works best.

I consider turkeys big game, and the calling options and strategies are complex. The well-equipped turkey bowhunter will have a special turkey vest or pack that contains box calls, slate/glass calls, diaphragm calls, push calls, etc. I have a lot to learn about turkey calling, but that's why I love it so much.

Moose are susceptible to calling, and while there may be a few moose calls on the market, you can get by with your mouth and some sort of homemade megaphone. By pinching your nose while cupping your hands over your mouth, you can imitate the nasal droning sound of a bull or a cow. Of course, you have to put yourself in the neighborhood of a rutting bull, and that is always the tough part. Using an old scapula (shoulder blade) or even a canoe paddle to scrape the brush and tree branches to simulate a bull raking a tree, can be even more effective than a call.

Rutting pronghorns can also be vocal. The bucks make a sort of squeaky snort that's difficult to describe. When a buck is cruising for does, and you're blind hunting with a decoy, an antelope call can be used to lure him into range.

That's not a complete list of big game species that can be lured into bow range with sounds. Woodland caribou in Newfoundland are extremely vulnerable to raking and rattling of antlers when they're rutting. Bears of all kinds can be called with predator calls, and a grunt or bleat may be the trick for pulling that big, rutting muley buck into range.

You just never know what will work. Keep an open mind and give yourself options. If you don't have the necessary audio tools in your pack, you'll never know what could have made a difference as the trophy of a lifetime walks away.

CHAPTER SEVENTEEN

The type of pack you use depends on the type of hunt. The further away you get from your camp or vehicle, the more gear you'll need. Because I carry lots of camera gear, I never use anything smaller than a daypack.

Packing Your Gear

"**G**ood grief! What ya got in this pack, gold?" I hear it all the time. My pack is heavy, 30 to 35 pounds, at all times. I'm so used to it, I don't even notice. Of course, when I watch some bowhunter take off through the woods with nothing but a bow in his hand and maybe a small fanny pack, I do get a bit jealous. I long for those fanny pack days.

Because I'm always carrying camera gear (listed in Chapter 21), my situation is different from the average bowhunter, who just has to carry hunting stuff. I need a pack that'll expand to handle all my gear, or contract if I need to ditch some stuff. Day two of a hunt is always "ditch" day, when unneeded gear gets tossed out.

I seldom carry a pack that'll hold less than 2,000 cubic inches. Currently, I'm using a Badlands 2200, because I've found it holds all my stuff and does it while riding relatively high on my back. I hate a pack that sags to the middle of my back.

A good pack is built with durable, relatively quiet material and quality zippers with large pulls that are easy to grab with gloves on. It should be lightweight yet have some integrity or body to it. It should also be designed by people who hunt. After all that, it comes down to deciding just how much pack you really need, keeping in mind, the bigger the pack, the more stuff you'll cram into it.

Let's look at the various sizes of packs and the logic for each.

For most hunts and hunters, a sizable fanny pack will do the trick. If it gets heavy, use a shoulder harness to distribute the weight between your shoulders and hips.

FANNY PACKS

Before I carried all that gear, I favored a fanny pack because it kept my gear on my hips and low so I could carry a treestand on my back. It was also easy to strap my fanny pack to my packframe loaded with elk meat. Occasionally, I used shoulder straps in conjunction with my fanny pack to distribute the weight between my shoulders and hips.

A fanny pack may be ideal for bowhunters who are seldom far from their vehicle, ie. whitetail hunters. Good fanny packs have plenty of room to carry a lunch, water, flashlights, knife, point-and-shoot camera, game calls, toilet paper, rope, and other necessary gear, plus some mechanism for strapping an extra fleece or a rain jacket to the top. Most bulky, heavy gear can be stored in your vehicle.

I still like a fanny pack, and if I didn't have so much to carry, I'd likely go back to one. Some good fanny packs designed for hunters include the Blacks Creek Kodiak Extreme, Horn Hunter Drop Tine, Badlands Nano, and Kifaru DayStalker. If your needs exceed the capability of a fanny pack but you're not willing to carry a full-sized daypack, consider the 8-Pocket Day Pack from Day One Camouflage. This pack is made of fleece and has pockets both inside and out that have elastic tops, so you can slip items in and out with deadly silence—the name of the game when hunting whitetails. Mine is big enough to haul almost all my gear and is the quietest pack I've ever used. I still use it in cold weather; however, this pack isn't waterproof, and once I added expensive camera gear I went to the Badlands pack. For many bowhunters, the Day One pack is an excellent option.

DAYPACKS

As you scale up your needs to day hunts in high country, away from camp or vehicle, your pack size may have to be scaled up as well. Something in the 2,000-cubic-inch range will handle most of the items you'll need for a long day in the field. In my pack I carry my hydration bladder (an extreme necessity on back-country hunts), all my emergency gear, tools, calls, cameras, tripod, GPS, and so on. I keep an emergency rain poncho in the bottom and strap extra layers of fleece to the outside as necessary. Like most quality packs, there is excellent support for my back and hips, so I can carry the load without undue fatigue.

You'll find no shortage of options, but look for a pack designed by hunters who have "been there done that." You'll want lots of outside pockets that allow you to slip a grunt call or rattle bag in and out without hassle or noise. A compartment for a hydration bladder puts your water comfortably on your back. When whitetail hunting, your pack and drink tube can be situated for a no-commotion sip. When hunting on the ground, you'll be able to stay hydrated by having easy access to your water. Just taking a swig, instead of dropping your pack and digging out your water bottle, helps keep the water flowing.

I also like the ability to strap my bow to my pack, so my hands are free to carry a blind, decoys (sometimes two), a tree-stand, steps, extra clothes, whatever.

Other high-quality packs in this size

A good daypack for high-country hunts will be strong enough to handle other tasks such as hauling antlers, cape and meat.

range are the Kifaru Spike Camp (2,300 cu. in.), Eberlestock Halftrack (2,300 cu. in.), Fieldline Big Buck Day Pack (2285 cu. in.), Horn Hunter MAINBEAM pack from Sportsman's Outdoor Products (2,050 cu. in.) and Blacks Creek Bone Collector 2.5. Obviously, these are not the only options, but if you look these packs over, you'll get a good idea of the quality and design you'll want in a pack. You'll have to factor in your budget, but again, this is not a place where you want to get tight with the hunting fund.

QUICK TIPS

- A whitetail hunter's pack should be a quiet one. Get one with quality zippers that don't make noise. The fabric should be quiet, even in cold weather, and there should be a strong loop or handle on top for hanging your pack on a treestep or limb. Because my pack is heavy with expensive gear, I hang it from both the strap on top and one shoulder strap.

- If your needs only include several calls, rangefinder, extra release, gloves, flashlight, and a few of the other essentials, you might get by with a Primos BowHunter's Vest. The pockets are designed for bowhunters, and the vest features a hole in the back for your safety harness tether. Just hang it up at the end of the day, and all your stuff is ready to go in the morning.

- Most packs come with lots of extra length on the straps. Cut off the excess, keeping in mind you might have to wear the pack over lots of clothes in cold weather. Now, make sure those strap ends are secure and not blowing in the wind when you're up in a bare tree.

- If your pack is not waterproof, make sure you store your camera (you do always carry one, right?) in a Ziploc bag or equivalent. However, plastic bags are noisy, so squeeze all the air out before closing.

- I consider a hydration bladder a necessity, but here's another advantage. As you drink the bladder shrinks, so there's no sloshing noise as there is with a half-empty bottle. Did I say I hate noise?

- If you don't have a hydration bladder, carry a small water bottle with a pull-up top because they create less commotion than screwing off a cap and you don't have to worry about dropping it. Also, a clear water bottle shines and sparkles in the sun, a nice black one doesn't.

- If your pack won't hold your bow, get a bowsling like the one made by Primos. You can secure your bow to the sling, throw it over your shoulder and behind you while you carry other items.

- Choose a pack that's made with a waterproof, or at least water resistant, material. The good ones have covered zippers to prevent water intrusion. You never know when you might get stranded, and you need to know the gear in your pack will stay dry.

- I prefer a pack with a profile narrower than my torso. That way I can slip through the woods without my pack hanging up on branches. I also like one that rides high on my back but not so high it grabs every branch I duck under.

- The best packs have special foam pads that ride on your back and hips yet allow air to circulate and help sweat evaporate. This is a very important feature on warm weather hunts for elk and mule deer.

- I also like packs that can be converted to carry meat, capes, and antlers. My Badlands 2200 has a "meat shelf" stored in the bottom. It's blaze orange and can be strapped over the top of a head and antlers or a boned-out elk quarter. That kind of versatility can save you a trip when recovering game. I have also emptied my pack, and the boned-out hindquarter of a bull elk fits in there nicely.

- Whitetail hunters should check out a unique pack called the BowBat by Game Plan Gear. The BowBat is a pack that wraps around your bow, then your stand tree once elevated! It contains all sorts of pockets and compartments for your essentials.

LARGE PACKS

When planning to carry your camp on your back, you'll have to go with a much larger pack. Hiking five miles into the backcountry on a bivouac hunt for elk will demand a very large pack with lots of structural integrity, comfortable back padding, and a high quality padded hip belt so you can distribute the weight. You'll need lots of space, probably a pack in the 4,000-cubic-inch-and-above range with lots of compartments and straps on the outside for attaching various items. Some good options are the Badlands 4500 (4,800 cu. in.), Kifaru LongHunter Standard (5,200 cu. in.), Eberlestock J107 (5,425 cu. in) and the Fieldline Dwight Schuh Mega Pack (5600 cu. in.).

These high-quality packs are designed to accommodate the serious bivouac bowhunter. Some are complex pieces of gear that will hold all your carefully chosen equipment, fit comfortably on your body, and hold up to serious abuse. A cheap pack won't do any of those things, and you'll suffer by scrimping here.

As mentioned at the beginning of this book, we won't get into actual camping

If your hunt demands lots of gear, a large pack of 4,000 square inches or more may be needed. Australian bowhunter, Damain Zeinert, brought a lot of gear along for his Quebec caribou hunt. Note his preference for footwear – tennis shoes!

and bivouac gear, as that's an entire book in itself. But rest assured, if you dive into that arena of hunting, you'll need a high-quality pack like those I've mentioned.

In summary, a well-built pack of any size, that's designed by people who have actually spent time in the field learning our needs and solving problems, is invaluable. Much of the gear we've discussed thus far is going to get left back on the kitchen table if you don't have something to carry it in.

There's nothing I hate worse than needing something and not having it. I suppose that explains why my pack weighs 35 pounds!

CHAPTER EIGHTEEN

Decoying big game is very entertaining. This buck couldn't stand the insolence of a doe that wouldn't submit, and he rammed her. Hitting the plastic decoy was quite a surprise as evidenced by his departure.

Decoying whitetails during the rut is a blast. When possible, the ultimate setup is two decoys — one a buck, the other a doe. Set them up in bow range and get ready for action!

Decoying Big Game

Evidently, she was really, really ugly. I couldn't think of any other reason why the 5x5 whitetail buck would drive his antlers into the chest of my doe decoy! He'd walked 50 yards through the woods just to check out the fake deer, but instead of walking up to the hind end of the doe, as you would expect a rutting buck to do, he faced her head-on.

I readied my camera and, after a short stare-down, the buck lowered his head and smashed into the decoy, knocking it backwards with a resounding plastic-like crashing noise. Stunned, the buck ran off to about 40 yards, then stopped and looked back at the discombobulated doe. The look on his face said, "Dang, I killed her!"

I laughed about that encounter but also tried to learn something about whitetail behavior. Granted, had I wanted to kill that buck, there were plenty of shot opportunities. Instead, I was trying to figure out why the buck assaulted the doe? I can only surmise that her unwillingness to divert her eyes or submit to his dominance was more than the buck could stand, and he wanted to put her in her place.

The observation and study of the interaction between the real thing and the copy is one of the most enjoyable aspects of hunting with a decoy. Speculating about the motivation behind that interaction and trying to answer the questions is part of the game. Never just accept the behavior of any animal without trying to understand it. Understanding game will make you a better bowhunter.

I spend quite a bit of my hunting time using a decoy, and not just for whitetails, but for antelope and elk, and even for moose and caribou. Decoying is entertaining, and that's my primary motivation for bowhunting in the first place.

Using a decoy is also a hassle to some degree, but I've always felt the disadvantages are outweighed by the advantages. Here are some thoughts.

WHITETAILS

Decoying whitetails is a little different from other species. You're actually trying to get the deer "up close and personal" with the decoy. I've had three attacks on my decoys over the years, and I'm anxiously awaiting the next one. Reaching this goal often requires a fairly realistic decoy. Fortunately, the decoy market is responding, and there are more options today than ever.

Three-dimensional decoys require more effort, but their realism is the pay-off. I started off with a Flambeau Redi-Doe that I modified by installing glass eyes I obtained from my taxidermist. I think these ultra-realistic eyes add life to the decoy, especially at close range.

I've also used Delta decoys extensively, because they're made of target foam and are quieter to haul and assemble in the field. Other decoys I've used are the Carry-

Lite and BuckWing Bob-n-Head decoy. The latter has both a head and tail that will bob around in a breeze and really draw attention. At this writing, Primos Hunting Calls is also in the process of introducing a decoy that uses the same principle. Flambeau's new Boss Buck decoy is extremely realistic but is just a bit large for my taste. It would take a very dominate buck to have the nerve to confront that decoy.

Two-dimensional decoys are also effective. In fact, I've seen bucks get really confused about the sudden disappearance of a flat decoy when they see it from the edge. They can also look very realistic in the right situation. Montana Decoys, which makes decoys out of fabric stretched over spring steel frames, has a buck that looks really good from a distance and offers other poses such as a feeding doe. Renzos Decoys are made of a weather-proof plastic material and have photo-real-

Two-dimensional decoys are light, easy to carry around, and very effective in fooling big game animals.

istic images of both bucks and does.

Portability is the primary advantage of this style of decoys. You can carry one or several with very little effort and without creating much noise. Set them up at different angles so at least one is visible at all times.

Everyone has their own decoying philosophy, and here's mine. In the pre-rut, when bucks are working out the pecking order for the upcoming rut, I like to use a buck decoy, preferably a bit smaller than the buck I'm hoping to encounter. This can upset the current pecking order and prompt a buck to set things straight. At this time of year bucks will be more interested in other bucks than does, so take advantage of that by also doing some rattling and grunting.

Once the chase phase of the rut arrives, I like to use two decoys by adding a doe. Yes, that is a serious hassle, especially when using 3-D decoys, but it's worth it to me. Setting up both a buck and a doe decoy is very effective. Not only does my buck challenge a cruising buck's turf, but he also has the nerve to have a doe with him. That's usually too much insolence for a buck to tolerate.

The nuances to decoying deer are numerous, but here's a word of caution: Does do not like decoys. They will invariably get nervous around a decoy, and that can cause problems. If a doe that's being pursued by a buck spooks at the sight of your decoy and runs off with the buck in tow, don't get discouraged and banish your decoy to the garage rafters. A decoy is not foolproof and will occasionally cause a negative response, but more often you'll get shot opportunities at bucks that would have never come close otherwise.

PRONGHORN ANTELOPE

I love sitting in a ground blind and watching rutting pronghorns respond to a decoy. My hunting buddies and I take our antelope decoying seriously and have a lot of fun.

Only lately has there been a decent 3-D antelope decoy on the market, the

---

QUICK TIPS

- A deer can walk right past a stationary decoy and not see it, so some type of movement is beneficial. Attach a strip of white plastic garbage bag or a lightweight foam tail to the back end of the decoy. Even just a slight movement in the breeze will capture the attention of a cruising buck.

- Imparting movement to your decoy also seems to calm suspicious does. If electronics are legal in your state, try a device called a Tail-Wagger. It's battery-powered and wags a foam tail every few seconds. That seems to make the does relax, plus it attracts attention from long range.

- Never surprise a deer with a decoy by using it in tight quarters. Set up in open staging areas or even field edges where a buck can study a decoy from afar and make up his mind. If he just stumbles on it at close range in thick woods, he could spook.

- Decoys aren't just for the rut. When hunting food plots in the early season you can create an appearance of confidence by setting up several decoys out in the field. Two-dimensional decoys work very well here because you can easily carry several.

- When handling a deer decoy, wear rubber or latex gloves to keep your scent off the decoy. This is a close-range endeavor, and a quick whiff at the wrong time can hurt you.

- There are no absolutes but, as a rule, set up a doe decoy quartering away from you and a buck decoy quartering toward your stand. If shooting lanes are tight, set your decoy toward the opposite side you expect the deer to approach from, because you'll have to shoot before the two touch noses.

- Transporting decoys is a major consideration. I've strapped my bow to my pack and carried one decoy under each arm, and I've also used the carry bag that comes with some decoys. A wheeled deer cart or even an old golf cart can be very helpful in open terrain. Use them to get your treestand/blind and decoys to the point where you want to assemble the decoy and slip in quietly the last few yards.

- In the right situations you can leave your assembled decoy(s) in the field by stashing them in the grass. That saves on noise and commotion when setting up on your next hunt.

Carry-Lite. Previously, we made our own antelope decoys by modifying a McKenzie 3-D target. We hollowed it out to save weight, then installed glass eyes and real horns. A pronghorn's vision is so good we wanted all the realism we could muster.

We went one step further, installing a steel rod at the balance point and a stand so the decoy could rotate. Finally, we attached a string to one front and one back leg and ran the lines through the grass to the ground blind. From inside the blind, a pull on one string, while leaving slack in the other, makes the decoy spin around. This movement, even if it's slight, can draw the attention of a pronghorn buck from a half-mile away or more.

I've also had some fun with smaller bucks that come to the decoy. Once, when a buck was close and studying my decoy I spun the decoy so it appeared to look out into an alfalfa field. The live buck immediately looked out the same direction, and I busted out laughing!

One of my hunting buddies, a perfectionist extraordinaire, went the last mile and is using a full-body mounted antelope built on a base that can also be rotated from inside his Double Bull blind. He always gets his buck.

Typically, I try to set up my blind and decoy in areas where antelope are traveling frequently. That can mean the traditional waterhole, a well-used fence crossing or, a particular field where they're feeding. With some scouting you'll find a place where there just seems to be a lot of pronghorns around all the time.

Two-dimensional decoys, such as those made by Mel Dutton, Montana Decoys, Flambeau, and Renzo's Decoys, can work when hunting from a blind, but they're better suited for a more aggressive style of hunting, which I call "pursuit decoying." That's when you combine spot-and-stalk hunting with a 2-D decoy.

This type of hunt works best if you have a hunting buddy. One is the shooter and the other the decoyer/rangefinder. Simply put, you locate a buck, preferably a herd buck with a harem of does. Experience will help you recognize the right situation, but you're looking for a buck that's spending a lot of time running off challengers. If the herd is in table-top flat terrain, the odds will be against you. However, if the terrain offers enough relief to hide your approach until you're about 100 yards or so from the herd, it might work.

Sneak up to the point where the last rise in terrain is the only thing between you and the herd. Have your buddy get behind the decoy, which he's holding with one hand, and a laser rangefinder in the other. Nock an arrow and position yourself either directly behind your buddy or off to the side if there is some cover, such as sage brush.

When you're both ready, have him tip the decoy up and advance to the horizon. One of two things will likely happen. Either the buck and his herd will spook and

Hunting buddy Ron Cizek takes his antelope decoying seriously. He use a full-body mounted pronghorn buck built on a rotating stand. From inside the blind he can pull strings to make the decoy turn, which really attracts attention.

run off, or the buck will break from the herd and head toward the decoy. He might come slowly, or if he's in the right mood, he could come charging at full speed. This is when it gets exciting!

As the buck approaches, your buddy should be relaying yardages. If he keeps his head down, you can rise up and shoot right over the top of the decoy, using it as cover prior to the shot. Obviously, special care needs to be taken that your buddy stays down at all times.

You should be prepared to take longer shots and do it quickly! A buck will often run up to bow range and stop to study the situation. They seem to be confused easily and may hesitate while you draw and shoot. Another common scenario is the buck runs up fairly close, spooks, and trots back toward his herd only to stop — still within bow range. It's crucial that you continue all the way to full draw and stay there until the antelope is gone. If you let down when he first spooks and have to re-draw after he stops, he's probably going to bolt.

When you can't wait for the antelope to come to you, consider "pursuit decoying" by using a 2-D decoy and challenging rutting bucks. Tip up the decoy and draw quickly!

Granted, this is a low-percentage tactic, but it's very exciting and may create an opportunity that isn't there for the less aggressive bowhunter. I've even heard stories of guys getting knocked over by rutting bucks that slam into the decoy. That's up close and personal!

If you're not hunting the rut, which is typically in mid-September, I'd stick to waterhole hunting. If the rut is on, a decoy will help you earn a shot opportunity.

ELK

Decoying elk is a different ball game, because you're not trying to get a bull to walk right up to a decoy. Your goal is much different.

In Montana, a decade ago, I was "guiding" my oldest son on his first elk hunt. I told him to set up on the lip of a deep draw and get ready.

"If an elk comes it will run into the bottom of that draw and come up to the top and be in bow range," I warned Jason. "Make sure you get to full draw while he's in the bottom, so you're ready when he pops up."

I slipped back 30 yards and set up a Feather-Flex foam elk decoy and let loose with a couple of cow calls. Before I could slip the call back into my pocket, a spike bull ran to the bottom of the draw, back up, and stood in front of a fully-drawn Jason at 15 yards! Brush obstructed his shot, and the bull was frozen in place.

QUICK TIPS

- Shoot the fastest bow you can. Pronghorns are lightning quick and can duck an arrow with ease.

- When hunting from a blind, set the decoy, whether it spins or not, within 20 yards of the blind. Pronghorns seldom worry about blinds as long as you don't move close to the shooting holes. Bucks are so intent on the decoy you can often get away with quite a bit of commotion prior to a shot.

- Wear all black in a blind, so you blend into the shadows.

- Shoot-through screen over the shooting holes isn't necessary for pronghorns. They're much more tolerant than whitetails of those black holes.

- Stay hydrated at all times. Take more water than you think you'll need, ration it, but make sure it's gone at the end of every day.

- Good binoculars are crucial, but I wouldn't bother with a spotting scope in a blind. You're essentially stuck there for the most part, and you'll see anything you need to see with a good pair of 10X binoculars.

- If you have a 2-D decoy, take it with you and lay it down out of sight behind the blind or inside. I've been caught inside a blind with a large herd buck running around over the hill and wishing I had a 2-D decoy so I could bail out of the blind and put the moves on him.

- If your 2-D decoy doesn't have a small oval-shaped hole in it, cut one so your buddy can range the incoming buck without exposing himself.

- If you're alone, pursuit decoying will be tougher, but it can be done. Your decoy will have to stand on its own while you shoot. Keep in mind, the ground in antelope country is very hard and you'll need sharp, strong stakes than can penetrate it. Stay behind the decoy until the last second, then rise up, draw, and shoot!

- Knee pads are invaluable for this type of hunting. The leather kind used by construction workers work well, because they stop cactus thorns. Leather gloves will also protect your hands to some degree.

I quickly cow-called again. The bull spotted the decoy and immediately walked toward it. Jason killed his first bull at seven yards. That day, at that moment, he thought his dad was a genius. I never corrected him.

When a bull elk responds to a call, whether it's a cow call, bugle, or just raking, it fully expects to see another elk. I can't think of anything, other than an errant breeze, that has ruined more elk encounters than this phenomenon. When that bull cannot spot another elk, the red flag of suspicion pops up. Every elk hunter knows what happens next – the bull starts to drift downwind and it's over.

A decoy can prevent that scenario from unfolding. I've mostly used that Feather-Flex decoy, which was a piece of lightweight foam air-brushed to look like an elk. Set up in the sun, this decoy was very realistic and was just enough to get an elk to say, "Oh, there it is." And, because the decoy didn't have a head, the bull had to determine the gender of the elk it was looking at. It never hurts to create questions that need answering.

That decoy isn't available anymore, but Montana Decoys makes an elk decoy that works on the same principle and is very lightweight and easy to carry and set up. Don't expect an elk decoy to be foolproof. You only need it to make a bull believe in your ruse and slip just a few yards deeper into your ambush.

OTHER SPECIES

I've used a similar decoy when moose hunting in Canada and can't say I had a bull actually see the decoy, but I'm betting it will work very well in the right situation. Moose are particularly susceptible to the "mental fog of the rut," and a decoy of any kind could easily pull a bull into bow range. Heck, a rutting bull moose will go after cattle, horses, and even pickup trucks, so a dark-colored decoy should work great in the bush.

Montana Decoys sent me a prototype caribou decoy, which I used in Quebec in 2007. Like all their decoys, it was very light, collapsible, and photo-realistic. I only

My oldest son, Jason, with his first elk, a tasty spike bull that came to a decoy.

- When setting up on elk, avoid ridges or hilltops. A responding bull will invariably come to the crest of the hill to scan the timber. That exposes only his head and neck, and you'll have no shot.

- Set up an elk decoy behind you or have your partner, who is doing the calling, set it up to attract a bull's attention and draw the bull past you.

- Set the decoy up in sunlight to increase visibility. Obviously, both caller and shooter should be in the shadows.

- You could attach a cow estrus scent wafer to a decoy, but if a bull gets downwind of it the encounter is probably over. I don't bother with scents, because I plan to get an arrow into a bull before he smells anything out of the ordinary.

- Most elk decoys are lightweight and easy to carry, but the real key is to use your decoy. It takes discipline to set it up every time you call, but it can't work if you don't set it up. And the first time you neglect to set it up, you know what will happen!

Set up an elk decoy in the sun for better visibility. Since you're not expecting a bull to walk right up to it, place it behind you.

had it for a week, but there was one situation where the decoy was beneficial.

We'd hit the migration perfectly the very first day of our hunt. The caribou were streaming past us in groups of 10 to 20 animals and, like all migrating caribou, they weren't interested in slowing down or stopping to allow for an ethical bow shot. Taking a shot at a walking animal at 30 or more yards is not a good idea so, in an effort to stop the caribou, at least momentarily, I set the decoy up in their path.

Most of the groups that came by stopped to study the decoy, which I'd set up about 50 yards out. The caribou walked between us and the decoy and, most importantly, they were looking the other way. None of the bulls that came by that day were "shooters," so I cannot say we killed a bull using the decoy. That said, we could easily have taken a number of bulls that were slowed and distracted by their fake brother.

Where do I start with turkeys? In recent years, a fully-mounted turkey decoy has proven to be the ultimate weapon, but they're expensive, unwieldy, and fragile. Does their effectiveness outweigh the hassles? Only you can decide that.

Otherwise, you'll have to choose from the myriad choices of turkey decoys from hens to jakes to gobblers. I've had excellent success with the Primos B-Mobile decoy. I inserted the feathers from one of my gobblers into the tail fan holder and it has brought the gobblers running toward a confrontation. The Pretty Boy from Knight & Hale is another one that works well if you're in the market for a gobbler decoy.

Hen decoys are important weapons in your turkey hunting arsenal too, and there are many options. Some fold up nicely in your pack and some are more realistic than others. Like calls, it pays to have several options and let the gobblers tell you which decoy they like best.

Since I possess neither the expertise nor space to expand on the nuances of turkey decoying, I'll leave you with one thought before moving on to the next chapter.

Fooling a game animal is really the essence of why many of us hunt. We strive to learn the idiosyncrasies and habits of the game we seek. What we learn can also show us the weaknesses we can exploit. It's that chess game that excites me. Working a decoy into my strategy of deception is one of the things I love most about bowhunting.

I tested a prototype caribou decoy in 2007. It's great for stalking, and I used it to coerce fast-moving migrating caribou to pause for a look.

My grandson, Carson, poses with my gob-
bler and a very effective turkey decoy to
which I affixed a real tail. Decoying turkeys
is deadly in most cases.

CHAPTER NINETEEN

*Bowhunting is an endeavor fraught with details,
the smallest of which can determine success.
Making sure a tiny twig doesn't get in the way of
your arrow is one of those details.*

Devil's in the Details

"**D**id you see that bull moose?"

"Yeah, he came in to about 80 yards but that was it," I replied to my hunting buddy, a well-known writer, as he walked out of the Newfoundland bush onto a gravel road.

"I thought he was going to come right . . . THUNK!"

The sound of something dropping to the gravel interrupted my buddy in mid-sentence. We both looked down, and there lay half his bowsight in the dirt. A compression bolt had worked loose, and the sight guard and pins slipped out.

Neither of us had a set of hex wrenches along to reattach the sight. He'd had the foresight to mark the position of the windage and elevation on his sight, but without a way to tighten it down, he was carrying a club.

Had we just left the road for the morning hunt, or if the sight had fallen off without his knowledge, he could have drawn on that moose only to discover he was suddenly hunting barebow!

We both had hex wrench sets in our bow cases back at the lodge, which is a really dumb place for such an important tool. Since that day, I never hunt without a set in my pack. I use it to check the tightness of bolts from time to time, and it's always there in case I ever lose something off my weapon.

It's the details that can hurt you. Bowhunting is strewn with "little things" that can make or break an encounter, a weekend hunting trip, or an expedition to the other side of the planet. Overlooking the tiniest detail can mean real trouble. If you take nothing else from this chapter, realize the importance of details both big and small.

I've broken things into sub-chapters for easy reference. You'll find lots of Quick Tips, but I certainly don't know them all. I'm still learning daily, which is why this book can never really be complete. These pages may cause you to think of tips of your own. If so, write them in the margins or in the blank pages in the back of this book for future reference.

HANDY TOOLS

Besides that all-important hex wrench set, you might consider a few other tools to stash in your pack, home, or camp. One such item is a multi-tool. I'm still carrying a Leatherman my brother, Dave, gave me when he was in the Coast Guard on Kodiak Island. We once flew into a remote cabin to bowhunt deer, and the regulator for the kerosene stove was on the fritz. Had I not had my Leatherman to repair the regulator, we'd have endured some cold nights.

Whether you're hunting in a treestand or a ground blind, you'll need pruners to trim small twigs and branches obstructing your vision or arrow path. I love my Leatherman Vista Pruners, which include other tools like a knife, screwdriver, and a very sharp saw blade. Pruners are quieter than a folding saw (also a must-have in your pack) for trimming up your hunting site. Some excellent saws and pruners are sold by Ameristep, Gerber, and Primos.

QUICK TIPS

- A hand pruner with a ratcheting feature will more easily lop off thicker branches. You'll be surprised how much you'll use a pruner, even when preparing to take kill photos.
- Carry a folding saw in your pack, especially if you plan to run-and-gun with your treestand. It's handy for cutting serious branches or dropping small trees, with landowner permission, of course.
- Some folding saws come with optional bone saw blades. If you plan to dismember a bull elk or moose, you'll wish you had a bone blade, as wood blades don't work well on bone.
- I prefer the pruning saws with handles that telescope for long reach. Some have lopping pruner attachments operated by a pull-rope. These are a bit quieter than sawing but don't handle larger limbs.

No bowhunter's tool shed is complete without a telescoping pruning saw. When placing treestands, you may need to trim branches out of your reach. I've trimmed branches from my treestand, and directed my ground-based buddy to branches that were in my way. The greatest advantage is you can trim specific branches without having to cut down entire limbs, or even trees, just to get one annoying branch. I've been burned too many times by that one branch I didn't take out, so my policy is – if in doubt, cut it out!

LIGHTING THE WAY

I can't think of a single piece of gear I would hate to forget more than my light. Or shall I say lights. I never carry only one and sometimes have three in my pack. On some hunts, having a light may be a matter of life and death. On most, it's just slightly less important.

Years ago, while trailing a buck late into the night, I knelt down to dig something out of my pack. I heard something walking toward me and shined my flashlight to see a doe feeding in my direction. She was oblivious to the beam of my light, even when shined directly in her face. She did not react or even look at me as she stood on her hind legs to browse, 15 yards away!

I heard another deer coming and shined my light right into the face of a little 3x3 buck coming from the same direction. Still no reaction. Neither deer paid me any attention, so I quietly dug my camera and flash out of my pack with the intention of getting a close-up photo. When I turned on the flash unit, and it began to squeal as it charged up, I almost got trampled by two terrified deer.

The point of the story? I don't worry about my flashlight spooking game. The sound of you walking, your scent, or the sight of you, may spook game, but I don't believe the light alone will hurt you.

I'd like to find the person who invented LEDs and give them a big hug (hope it's a woman). LED headlamps and flashlights are invaluable to the bowhunter. Though most LED lights are not sufficient for bloodtrailing game, they are plenty good for everything else, including hiking in the dark, sorting through your pack, climbing trees, setting up decoys, laying down lure scents, signaling others, and keeping you from walking off a cliff, into a river, or poking yourself in the eye.

Because the filament of an LED is encased in resin, these "bulbs" are almost indestructible in hunting conditions. Their extreme efficiency means your batteries last many times longer than lights using incandescent bulbs. Combine those two qualities and you have a very dependable light source, as long as the other parts, such as the switch, are built tough.

I can't imagine hunting without an LED headlamp anymore. I use it without fear of spooking game, although I only use it when necessary. If the sky is moon-lit, I'm still wearing my headlamp so I can quickly turn it on if necessary. Once, in Montana's Musselshell riverbottom, I almost stepped on a porcupine in the dark but flipped on my light just in time to see what was rustling in the grass ahead of me!

I carry two headlamps, one ultra-small single LED model that runs on AAA batteries, and a spare with multiple bulbs and larger batteries for times when I need more light, such as field-dressing. If one headlamp dies for some reason (I have had trouble with switches on some models) I pull out the back-up.

I also carry a hand-held flashlight with either an ultra-bright LED or a Xenon bulb, so I have enough brightness for initial bloodtrailing. Also, if you're in a boat searching for camp, or scanning the forest floor for a dead body, you'll appreciate

I can't imagine a more popular invention in the outdoor world in recent years than the LED headlamp. They're durable, efficient, hands-free, and indispensable. But don't forget a back-up flashlight.

a light that throws a decent beam.

In my truck is a big Mag Light powered by D-Cell batteries. That baby throws a serious beam and is great for penetrating thick woods. Some lights are designed specifically for bloodtrailing and employ a colored lens intended to make blood stand out. One such light is the Primos Blood Hunter, and one of those is in my truck as well, along with the charger.

TACKLE BOX

Every bowhunter should have a tackle box in which to keep the myriad small items he'll need to maintain his bow and arrows. You don't necessarily need all the equipment necessary to set-up and tune a bow, but there are a few things you'll need to keep your weapon in hunting shape.

My tackle box contains the usual tools, such as a T-square and nocking pliers. I don't use nocking points anymore, just string loops, but I never know when I may need those two basic tools. You'll find string loop cord, scissors, and a lighter to melt cord ends. These items will help me repair any problems with my string loop.

pack. Lithium batteries are becoming more widely available, and they are lighter in weight and last longer than traditional batteries. Lithium is also more efficient in cold weather.

- Many LED headlamps come with colored lenses, and that's not by accident. Besides being less perceptible to game (at least we humans think so) the blue, red, and green lenses allow you to maintain your night vision, because your iris isn't having to work so hard to adjust to bright white light and then total darkness.

- Everyone's eyesight is different, and some people suffer from varying degrees of colorblindness, particularly in the red and brown range. You'll have to experiment with different lens colors to see what works best for you.

- For safety's sake, always wear a lit headlamp when hiking through the dark in woods and fields that hold other hunters. The light won't hurt you, and it's impossible for others to mistake you for an animal.

- If you're packing light or have a small pack, one of the LED lights that clip on the brim of a hat work great for most tasks; just don't count on them for bloodtrailing or to save your life in a crisis.

- Imagine finding yourself stranded on a mountain in the dark, all night long. How much would you pay for a good light then? Don't be cheap with your lights, buy the best you can find. Some good manufacturers include Petzl, Princeton Tec, Cyclops, Essential Gear, Cabelas, Surefire and others.

If you don't already have a tackle box of some kind, get one. You'll slowly fill it with all kinds of "stuff" that'll eventually qualify as junk. However, you'll need the essentials if you plan to maintain your own bow and arrows.

I also carry extra peep sights, plus a peep that uses rubber cord, just in case I have to do an emergency installation of a peep without having to worry about alignment at full draw. Serving thread is also important for many uses and is always in my tackle box.

A portable bow press is also useful if you plan to do some of your own work. The Ratchet-Loc Bow Press from Ram Products, Inc., and the Bowmaster, are two options. However, make certain a particular press works on your bow. There are so many configurations these days, some bows require a special press and some none at all.

String wax is an essential item for keeping your bowstrings and cables in good shape, and a little dab on the threads of your broadheads will keep them tight. Fletching glue will help you repair loose fletching, replace nocks, and anything else that needs gluing. I lean toward the cyanoacrylate (Super Glue) adhesives, because they're quick and strong. Goat Tuff Glue from Tim's Archery and Arizona Archery Products' Fastset Gel are two excellent adhesives.

A supply of arrow inserts, field points, practice broadheads, fresh blades or new broadheads, a broadhead wrench, and Judo points occupy one drawer in my box. A couple of plastic nock wrenches help me fine-tune the position of my fletching, and spare nocks can be glued on quickly.

Complete sets of hex wrenches, both in a folding tool and loose, are a must, and you'll end up with quite a collection after a of couple years. Loctite will keep your screws and bolts tight, and I have a compartment full of spare screws and bolts in case I lose one. A tape measure can be used to verify specific measurements, such as axle-to-axle length and brace height.

Adhesive fleece will quiet almost any noise imaginable. Hot melt glue is necessary for inserts in aluminum arrows. And a good marking pen will help you keep track of the precise placement of sights and arrow rests once they're set.

Extras, such as string dampening devices, cable slides, arrow rest, bowsight, stabilizer, mechanical release, and other items are good to have at your fingertips, provided your tackle box is big enough. If it isn't, you'll eventually end up with a bigger one – trust me.

TARGETS

Because archery is all about practice, I need to include a few words about targets. You'll find all sorts of targets to shoot at organized archery events such as 3-D tournaments and indoor shooting. That's not my focus here. As a bowhunter, you need a couple of targets at your disposal without having to drive 100 miles or wait for a tournament date. You must have the ability to practice according to your schedule.

If you live in an urban area, it may not be possible to shoot in your backyard. If it is, consider getting your own 3-D target such as a Glen-Del Buck or those made by McKenzie/Delta and Rinehart. These targets allow you to concentrate on shooting at realistic vitals instead of spot targets. You'll learn to pick a spot, and if you can set it up below a deck, treestand, or some elevated position (don't get on your roof) you can practice shots at a downward angle.

I would also recommend having a portable target in your vehicle, whether you're driving 10 miles from home or 2,000 miles. Throw the target out and take a few shots before going into the field. Not only will that expose any potential problems, such as a creak in your draw cycle, but it will give you supreme confidence when everything is clicking and your arrows are going where you point them. Good portables are the Block 4x4 Pup, Morrell Yellow Jacket, and the Rinehart 18-1.

QUICK TIPS

- At the very top of this list, at least for the whitetail hunter, is a bow holder. I use the Realtree EZHanger and never get in a tree without it. I like my bow hanging within easy reach, out in front of me if possible, so there's a minimum of commotion when I prepare for a shot. I put some fleece on the hook so there is nothing but silence when I grab my bow. Primos makes another good one.

- Carry a practice broadhead in your quiver at all times. Don't shoot arrows from your stand or you could spook unseen game, but take a practice shot as you walk in and out or whenever you have a safe backstop. A Zwickey Judo point works great in tall grass.

I won't hunt from a treestand without a bow hanger of some sort. It keeps my bow hanging in front of me, at the ready. Note the adhesive fleece on the hook to deaden any noise.

- Even if you don't need an armguard in the summer, get used to wearing one. In cold weather you'll need one to keep your jacket sleeve away from your bowstring.

- Face paint, or a lightweight mask, will cover your face, something that stands out in the woods like a neon sign. This is especially important when hunting on the ground. When elk hunting I wear face paint because a facemask is too warm and can inadvertently obstruct my vision.

- I buy a whole box of unscented baby wipes and split them up in several Ziploc bags, squeezing the air out before sealing. I use these for cleaning off face paint, washing my hair (I keep it short in the hunting season) and cleaning up a dead animal. They are also very nice to use after you've finished doing what bears do in the woods.

- Wrap some duct tape around an ink pen and keep it in your pack. It works great for covering hot spots on your feet before they become blisters, and there are a million other uses for this magical product.

- Take an old fleece shirt or similar camouflage material and make a tree bark cover. Cut it into a rectangle shape, then attach a stretch cord to the top and bottom. Once you're in your treestand, wrap the cord around the tree and tie it off so the fleece is between your back and the tree. This will prevent those annoying scraping noises when you stand and lean against the tree.

- If you hunt where there are bugs, get a ThermaCELL. This device uses butane (you cannot take it on an airplane) to heat up a scented pad that repels mosquitoes. It has become a must-have product for spring bear hunters and early season whitetail hunters. This product works!

- Keep some reflective tacks or tape in your pack or truck so you can mark a trail. If you're whitetail hunting you may want to slip in during the morning darkness or send a friend into a stand they couldn't find otherwise. Reflectors are also useful on elk hunts if you want to get to specific locations well before daylight or find an obscure trail in the dark on the way out.

- Try a hearing enhancement device such as a Walker's Game Ear. I have some hearing loss in my left ear from my young days behind a rifle, and my directional hearing is poor. I was quite impressed with what I was able to hear with a Game Ear. I don't like it in every situation, but when it's quiet they are a useful "early warning system."

If you plan to hunt where there are bugs you'll want a ThermaCELL unit. This device uses butane to heat a bug repellent pad. Bear hunters in Canada swear by them!

- Many archers use wrist straps on their bows. They offer some security when you hold your bow with a loose grip. If you decide to use one, get it well before the hunting season. You'll need to get used to it. I find the slight delay in getting my hand on the grip is something I don't need, but if you like them, go for it.

- In cold weather an aluminum bow grip can get very cold, even if it's just the front of the grip. Wrap your grip with a LimbSaver Tentacle Wrap or even just some rubber tape. Be sure to practice with this wrap, because it will change the way you grip your bow.

- Keep some pain relievers in your pack. I find Motrin will knock down any headache I get as well as inflammation. Keep in mind that Tylenol, or like products, will not relieve inflammation, just headaches. I also carry a few snacks so I can eat something with a Motrin. A bad headache, whether it's caused by dehydration or elevation, can stop you cold.

- Lighted nocks, such as the Lumenok, Firenock, or Easton's Tracer Nock, may be illegal in your area, and they are not accepted by the Pope and Young Club, but they will help you track arrow flight and recover your arrow.

- When hunting the West, you'll want some way to hang your bow so your hands are free to glass or call. A hook on your belt works well, as does a product called a Hip Clip. It's a small rubber device that captures your bowstring, and I've used it quite extensively. I attach it to the waist belt of my pack. Another option is a Balcom Hook and Sling, and Crooked Horn also makes a bow hook.

When hunting open country that requires periods of glassing, you'll want both hands free. Use some type of bow-holding device like a sling or maybe a Hip Clip. This handy device straps to your belt or pack, and your bow hangs by the string.

MISCELLANEOUS

This section is NOT a list of oddball items you don't really need. To repeat, bowhunting is always about the little things. The smallest detail can derail a year's worth of preparatory effort and transform a great hunt into a disaster. Think seriously about the following list of Quick Tips. There's some repetition here (for those who like to skip ahead), but any single detail could make a difference.

GAME CARE

Provided you've paid attention to details and your preparation was thorough, there's a good chance you'll end up standing over a dead animal that needs to be field-dressed. Of course, you'll have to take care of the photo session, but I've devoted an entire chapter to that, and it's coming up. Here we'll discuss some gear for game care.

A quality knife is one of those pieces of gear you can really get attached to over time. When I was 17 years old, I bought a Ka-Bar knife with the leather handle and long, straight blade. That knife followed me everywhere until recent years when the airlines started getting fussy about weight and knives in general. I don't carry it much anymore, but it's one of my most treasured possessions. It doesn't hold an edge all that well, but that means it's also easier to get sharp. I can't begin to count the big game animals I've taken care of with that knife.

In Montana, in the early '90s, a mountain lion stalked me (story in Chapter 11) as I called to a bull elk. With the lion crouched 18 yards away, staring at me, I

My trusty old Ka-Bar (top) has been with me since I was 17, and the blade does-n't look the same. Carry a simple, lightweight, ultra-sharp knife and maybe a diamond sharpener to keep it that way. The Sagen Saw will take care of the pelvic bone for you.

I consider handling the meat of the animals I kill a labor of love. It can be hard work, but for me, it just adds to the feeling of satisfaction I get from hunting for my food.

unbuckled the strap on my razor-sharp Ka-Bar knife and nervously grasped the handle. Had the lion attacked he may have killed me, but I assure you, I'd have hurt that cat real bad.

My knife is bigger than it has to be, and that makes it cumbersome to haul around. A better option is a folding knife, or a solid one that isn't too long and bulky. If it's razor sharp, any knife will work. I like a small, narrow blade for caping heads, so I don't have to haul the skull out of the bush. A medium-sized folding knife will handle your field-dressing duties and stores nicely in your pack. That's all you need when hunting whitetails around home.

Remote hunts are a bit more complicated. Warm weather is often a factor when hunting elk and moose, and because they're so large, you'll have a major task ahead of you. In those scenarios I carry some sort of sharpening tool, such as a diamond stick or stone, to tune up my knife. Carrying two freshly sharpened knives in your pack isn't a bad idea either. My Ka-Bar can't quite get through the field-dressing and skinning of a bull elk before it needs a tune-up.

Depending on the animal, and the room in your pack, a saw of some type can be very handy. A Wyoming Saw has both wood and bone blades and will make short work of an elk. Smaller saws, like the ultra-compact Sagen Saw, are great for splitting the pelvis on deer-sized game. Some folding saws, like the Gerber, also come with bone blades. Outdoor Edge Cutlery offers a full line of saws and knives.

Knowledge is a very important tool if you have to quarter or bone an elk, for example. I learned by helping my father-in-law butcher cows and hogs years ago. With a good knife and a saw I can reduce a bull elk to a very manageable size in short order. Everyone has their own way of doing things. Some like to gut the animal and work from there, others prefer to strip an elk of its meat without ever gutting it.

If you're alone, you'll likely need some stout rope, such as parachute cord, to tie legs off to trees or saplings while you work on the animal. Latex gloves are also a good idea for keeping your hands clean and warding off bacteria.

How you get to the next step is your choice, but eventually you'll need to protect your meat from flies. I like to carry those ultra-lightweight cheesecloth game bags, because they don't take up any room in my pack and I can stretch them over my meat to keep the flies off. I also stash the meat in the shade, paying attention to the sun's travel.

Hauling meat back to camp depends on the terrain, of course. If it's open and fairly flat terrain a deer cart works great for hauling out deer or even quarters and pieces of larger game. They're not much good in the high country, so you'll need horses or a strong back.

Another one of my most treasured possessions is my freighter frame. It's a simple aluminum pack frame with a shelf. Over the years, on many do-it-myself elk hunts, I've used my frame to haul out both my elk and those of my buddies. Back when I was young, dumb, and strong, I even strapped half a spike bull to my pack and hauled him out! Maybe that's why I'm slow to get going some mornings!

I prefer the separate pack frame and usually have to make a trip back to camp anyway. I generally strap the cape and antlers under the meat shelf on my Badlands pack for the first trip and then come back for the meat with my pack frame. That can take time, which is why you'll need to get your meat covered and in the shade before you leave.

It doesn't take a lot of tools or gear to get your animal to a processor. A sharp knife, a good packframe, and strong back will take care of most of the work.

FITNESS GEAR

It goes without saying that your body is your single most important piece of hunting gear. A fit body will make you a better bowhunter regardless of whether you're sitting all day in a whitetail stand or climbing into mountain goat country. In either of those scenarios, recovering your animal can be the most strenuous part of your hunt, and being in shape always helps in that regard.

Besides, staying in good physical condition will go a long way toward maintaining the strong shoulders, back, and healthy joints you'll need to keep drawing a

To improve my physical conditioning for a hunt, I like to strap on my pack frame with 40 lbs. of sand and hike in the hills. I carry my bow and practice my uphill and downhill shooting to keep the hike interesting.

bow for years to come.

Any sort of exercise will help, and you can take it to whatever level you feel comfortable. Just walking goes a long way, and running is good too, if you're young enough and fit enough to do it safely. It's always a good idea to see a doctor for a physical before starting any exercise program. Whether you walk or run, make sure you have the appropriate shoes.

I live in North Dakota, so walks in the winter are a bit nippy. I have a heavy duty treadmill in my basement and can walk or run, even on inclines to 12 degrees, at any time, in any weather. A stair climber is also very useful when preparing for a hunt in mountainous terrain, because it works all the leg muscles necessary for climbing.

QUICK TIPS

- It should go without saying, you should never start an exercise program without first consulting your doctor. Be realistic in your expectations. If you aren't sure you can get in good enough shape to handle a mountain goat hunt, look for another hunt you'll enjoy.

- Always start off slow and work your way into a more strenuous routine. Keep in mind, if you overdo it and injure yourself, your hunt may be over before it gets started.

- On my treadmill, I start off walking on level ground then gradually increase the incline. You'd be surprised how much a 12-percent grade will work your body. I'll also do some running to stretch my lungs.

- As my hunt approaches, I wear a pack frame with 40 pounds of sand strapped to it as I walk on the treadmill. That gets my shoulders, back, and legs used to the extra weight. I also carry eight-pound dumbbells in both hands so my arms and shoulders get accustomed to carrying a bow.

- If you have access to weights, they can help strengthen all parts of your body, but be careful you don't overdo it.

- Of course, there's nothing like working out in the field, so it's a good idea to find some hilly ground and test your body and your boots before a strenuous hunt.

- Losing weight is a major part of improving your physical condition. Most of us can afford to lose a few pounds. It takes discipline to diet, but you'll see much better progress if you're exercising at the same time. If you want to play, you have to pay.

Another piece of fitness gear that is important to the bowhunter is an item called the Bow Fit. It's an elastic tube with a handle that simulates your bow. It's adjustable to the length of your draw. You pull the tube to your anchor, working the muscles in your back, shoulders, and arms in the same manner as drawing your bow. Use this handy device to warm up before a practice session or to keep in shooting shape when you can't get to an archery range.

Have I forgotten anything?

There's no doubt about it.

I've racked my brain silly trying to remember every little thing that could affect your bowhunting efforts. The minute I send this book to the publisher I'll think of dozens of more details. Still, I hope you've gleaned some ideas from these first 19 chapters, and if you think of any more, let me know.

I can't get enough bowhunting details.

CHAPTER TWENTY

Traveling bowhunters will find themselves in scenes like this, packed up and ready to go. But will your gear arrive on time and in good shape? If you take care of business, the answer will be "yes" on both counts.

The Traveling Bowhunter

The feeling could only be described as sickening. Much like the current of a lazy river, the airport baggage carousel slipped past slowly, methodically, and empty! Every other traveler had left, and I stood there with hunting buddy Larry D. Jones and only my duffel bag beside me. Larry had all his gear. The only thing missing was my bow case!

Amplifying the agony was the fact that we were waiting at the airport in Auckland, New Zealand! Within a few hours we'd be flying on to Queenstown for a red stag hunt in one of the most beautiful places on this planet.

I'd already been to the oversized baggage department, and my bow case wasn't there either. It didn't make the trip across the pond from San Francisco.

The two-hour flight to Queenstown was breathtaking, but even a bird's-eye view of those spectacular mountain ranges couldn't erase the nagging feeling my bow case might not show up. The airlines assured me my bow would be delivered to Queenstown the next day, but I was skeptical.

Fortunately, Larry and I had planned for just such a scenario by arriving a day early. We spent our layover time wandering the streets of Queenstown, a beautifully quaint resort community on the shore of Lake Wakatipu.

Though I was worried about my bow case arriving, I was not concerned whether my two bows would be in good condition when, and if, they finally arrived. They were protected by my SKB bow case. Even airport baggage handlers couldn't hurt my gear.

You can imagine my relief at 11 a.m. the next morning when I saw my bow case in the baggage claim office at the Queenstown Airport! It was time to go hunting!

A traveling bowhunter must take many things into consideration prior to a trip. When driving a vehicle there are few problems, because you can take everything you need and even pull a trailer if necessary. Even in a vehicle it's still a good idea to store your bow or bows in a hard case, because things get bumped or piled-on, and damage could result. Other gear such as clothing can simply be stuffed into rubber tubs or duffel bags.

Traveling by air is a completely different animal. Airline regulations are changing constantly and you must keep abreast of the rules. It wasn't long ago you were allowed 70 pounds per bag on international flights, but that's gone away. Now the limit is one or two pieces of luggage, each with a weight limit of 50 pounds. They will weigh your bags and, depending on the agent, may even make you take a couple pounds out.

In addition, you'll be allowed a carry-on bag that must fit in the overhead baggage compartment. Many air travelers push the envelope when it comes to carry-on baggage, but you're better off to keep it small so you don't run into problems. I use my daypack as my carry-on bag, and it contains all my valuables, such as optics and cameras.

BOWHUNTING LUGGAGE

I do a lot of traveling, and the best thing ever invented is the wheeled duffel. Trying to lug a 50-pound bag through a giant, busy airport isn't fun. There are usually carts available, but I prefer to be independent. A wheeled duffel with a pull-out handle lets me cruise through parking lots and airport terminals with ease.

I don't recommend a camouflage duffel, because you never know who is handling your baggage. There's no sense confirming to those behind the scenes that the person who owns the bag is a hunter. I'm not saying some anti-hunting type could cause your bag to be delayed (they wouldn't do that, would they?) but I do know my bow case gets lost more often than my duffel bag.

I've been using a Cabela's Alaskan Guide XL wheeled duffel for a long time, and it has held up well. There are many options, but do not get a giant bag big enough to haul a dead body. You'll just be tempted to pack it full and end up paying excess baggage fees. My bag's dimensions are 36" x 16" x 18" and it gives me all the room I need. In fact, when it weighs 50 pounds there is still plenty of room, depending on what's inside. If I need to haul a sleeping bag with me, it fits with ease.

My bag also has a bottom compartment where I stash my boots, pack tripod, safety harness, and

When choosing a bow case consider the treatment it will receive and be sure to get a double-bow case so you have extra room even when carrying just one bow. You may even opt for a soft case like those on the left.

other such items. Cabela's has other models, including one that's waterproof. Some excellent wheeled duffels are made by Columbia, Badlands, Blacks Creek, and others, but my bag is a good example of simplicity that works.

BOW CASES

My first piece of advice here is to get a double bow case, even if you only travel with one bow.

I always take two bows on hunting trips. I used to carry extra strings and a portable bow press, as well as other stuff I needed to reassemble or tune a bow. I now take a back-up bow, because time is always short on a hunt. Rather than spend a day getting a bow tuned, I'd rather just grab my back-up bow out of the case and go hunting.

Whether you agree or not, a double bow case is a good idea. Because of the 50-pound weight limit, it doesn't make sense to get a single bow case that when filled to capacity weighs only 35 pounds. You'd be cheating yourself out of 15 pounds, because you can't put the extra weight in your duffle. You can still pack one bow in a double case and end up with all sorts of extra room for clothing and other gear. You might as well pack each bag to 50 pounds, because you're paying for it.

One thing you'll have to pay attention to when choosing a bow case is its empty weight. It counts against your total, so if a hard case weighs 25 pounds empty, that only leaves 25 pounds for bows, arrows, and other gear.

I've used SKB cases for a number of years and started off with a double bow case, but the newer parallel limb bows no longer fit. I solved the problem by switching to their Parallel Limb Bow Case (model 4114A) and would have converted anyway because it has wheels! I can wear my daypack, grab my bow case in one hand and my duffel in the other, and I'm mobile and agile.

Another feature I like about my bow case is the locks are TSA approved. That means the security folks at airports have a key that fits the locks. I can lock my case before I check my baggage and know it will be locked when I pick it up, even if the security folks look inside, and they almost always do. Of course, this doesn't necessarily apply in foreign countries.

Some very good bow cases are also made by Kalispel Cases, Vanguard, Plano, Doskocil, Lakewood, and Flambeau. Some are lighter than others, and that will save you room for gear. The trade-off is the level of protection from potential abuse.

My case weighs 20 pounds empty. That leaves me 30 pounds to work with, and though that doesn't sound like much, it is. A fully-outfitted bow, without arrows, can weigh from five to eight pounds. If you carry two, which I always do, that's about 14 pounds for two bows. Eighteen 400-grain arrows weigh about one pound, so arrows are a non-factor. Broadheads weigh even less.

I recommend using your daypack as your carry-on bag when flying. Stow all your valuables, including optics, cameras, rangefinder, passport, boarding passes, etc., and don't let the pack out of your sight for any reason.

The rest of the available weight, about 15 pounds, can be taken up by things you don't want in your duffel or carry-on, like mechanical releases that can look like a gun barrel on X-rays.

TIME TO PACK

Here's how I pack my bow case, which I do first. My case has a foam arrow holder that's backed up against the edge, so I load it with arrows. I generally take anywhere from a dozen to 18 arrows along, depending on the type of hunt. Not necessarily because I think I'll shoot that many, but there could be some type of accident, especially around horses, that could wipe out an entire quiver full of arrows. I don't take chances with such critical gear.

Because I never know if both bags will show up, I like to use one set of hunting clothing as packing material in my bow case. I'll lay a set of high-tech undergarments, such as Under Armour, in the bottom of my case, then lay one bow on top of that. Next, I wrap a fleece pullover or some mid-layer garment around the strings, cables, and cams of that bow to protect them from chafing.

Every nook and cranny at either end of the case is packed with various items like my homemade broadhead container, two releases tucked inside gloves so they don't rub on things, folding knife and stabilizer inside socks, lights, calls, Ziploc bags with bow maintenance items like string wax, serving thread, and any other miscellaneous items such as spare batteries, baby wipes, etc. I'll slide some things under the buss cables, like my hydration bladder for my pack, but nothing sharp or abrasive.

Then I start adding layers of hunting clothes like camo pants and shirt on top of the bow, with extra layers over the sight and rest. The second bow is positioned over those clothes, usually offset so the sights don't overlap. The final layer is a jacket or heavy fleece of some kind, just in case my duffel doesn't show up for a day or two.

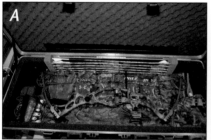

A.) Pack your bow case by starting off with a layer of clothing, then your back-up bow. Fill in spaces with other gear like broadheads, quiver, etc. B.) With a layer of camouflage pants and shirt between, add your primary bow, offset so accessories don't conflict. C.) Fill all the gaps with other gear, then cover your primary bow with outer clothing so you have a complete outfit. Now make sure it all weighs less than 50 pounds!

Quiver parts are slipped into heavy socks or facemasks, and my "kill hat," a Bowhunter Magazine cap, goes on top. I fill the voids with spare gloves and other soft items and then try to close the case. If it closes, I weigh it. If necessary, I'll cut back on the clothing I've stuffed in to get to my weight limit. My goal is 49 pounds, to allow for some leeway between my scale and the airline's.

Everything else I need goes in my duffel, including more clothes, both hunting and "civilian," rainsuit, boots, camp shoes (if I'm not wearing them on the plane),

QUICK TIPS

- Some traveling bowhunters prefer to use thick, heavy duty soft cases for their bow(s), and that seems to work for them. Personally, I don't trust baggage handlers that much, and I will always opt for a hard case. It's your call.

- Removing the padding from the interior of some hard bow cases can give you more room to use hunting clothing as padding.

- If your hunt includes riding horseback or stuffing your gear into a float plane, you may be instructed to bring a soft case for your bow. Hard cases are bulky and difficult to pack into tight places. A quality soft case that isn't too bulky can be stuffed into your duffel.

- If your bow case doesn't have TSA locks, you can get padlocks that are TSA approved. TSA agents will have keys for inspection.

- You could buy an arrow case, or you could make one. Take a piece of 3" PVC and cut it two inches longer than your arrows. Get two caps and glue one on. Shove a one-inch-thick piece of ethafoam in the end of each cap. Make two half-inch-thick slices of ethafoam and drill quarter-inch holes in both slices held together. Mine has 18 holes, and I feed half my arrows from each direction, spread out the two slices, position the fletching so they don't touch, then slide the whole works into my tube. It's virtually indestructible.

- Even if you don't have a trip planned now, get your passport. You never know when an international hunt, and that includes Canada, may pop up. You won't get a passport on the spur-of-the-moment.

- If you're traveling with a buddy, split up your back-up bows, half your arrows, broadheads, quivers, and spare releases. That way, if only one case shows up, you can still hunt.

- You can apply the previous strategy to your duffel as well. Split your clothing in half and place in a bag or stuff sack. Put half in your duffel and half in your buddy's.
- If you reload shotgun or rifle shells, or handle muzzleloaders, do not handle any of your bowhunting gear or luggage before thoroughly cleaning up. The gun powder residue can show up on the swipes taken by TSA agents, and you'll likely miss your flight!

travel kit, and plenty of socks and underwear. If my duffel ends up weighing 49 pounds or less, I'm good. If I'm short on either bag, I'll add the borderline items I'm debating about taking along like a portable bow press, different style boots, and so forth. However, I'm usually overweight and end up trimming my clothing supply. We all have a tendency to take too many clothes because we're trying to adjust to varying conditions. This is yet another reason why layering is so efficient.

Finally, I pack my daypack, starting off with cameras, flash, batteries, binoculars, rangefinder, reading glasses, notebook and pen, and any item I think someone might like to pilfer from my checked luggage. In one zippered pouch I keep my passport, itinerary, and boarding passes, so I always know where they are. Things to avoid are knives, multi-tools, releases, duct tape, broadhead parts, liquids, gels, and anything else that makes airport security agents nervous.

If you don't have room for arrows in your bow case, you can make your own arrow tube with PVC and stuff it in your duffel bag.

Your daypack should never leave your sight unless it's in the overhead compartment above you on the plane. If you leave the plane due to a delay for some reason, do not leave your pack. A friend of mine did that en route to an Alaska moose hunt and when he came back the plane was gone! Your carry-on is your baby, treat it that way.

Because my daypack is always in my possession, I don't concern myself with it being camouflaged. Anti-hunting types may not like it, but I don't care what they think. If you conduct yourself respectfully and dress appropriately, non-hunters won't care. You might just show them not all hunters are beer-swigging, blood-spilling buffoons.

Wherever you're traveling, I would ask you to represent the rest of us with class. When traveling by air, make sure you get to the airport at least 90 minutes in advance. Sure, small airports aren't a problem, but if you're hoping to get your baggage checked, inspected, and through security in a major airport in less than an hour, you're being optimistic. Missing a flight can really snowball into a major problem and could ruin your hunt. Don't take chances; be early.

If your bow case doesn't show up at baggage claim, it's more than likely at the oversized baggage office. Most airlines treat large bags like bow and firearm cases, golf bags, and skis differently, because they may not ride well in the baggage carousel. I believe this also leads to a higher incidence of my bow case not showing up on the same plane.

Again, make sure you stay abreast of all the airline travel rules and plan ahead. Traveling to bowhunt faraway places can be very stressful, but once you're there the excitement will make you forget your troubles.

Taking photos of taking photos is the epitome of the effort necessary to preserve your hunt memories. Be sure you take the time to do things right.

Capturing the Memories

I used to subscribe to the theory that my memories were the one thing no one could ever take away from me. I was wrong. My father was stricken with Parkinson's Disease, and as if that weren't enough, he was diagnosed with a brain tumor and passed away as I wrote this book. He never hunted, but his memories of the times my brother Dave and I spent fishing with him over four decades were gone. It could happen to any of us.

This realization makes my memories even more precious and increases my resolve to preserve them in any way I can. If I make it to old age, and let it be known I'm resisting that in every possible way, I'll be able to cling to the memories of the time I spent in the outdoors with my dad, sons, grandsons, and other relatives and friends.

Being an outdoor writer for the past 26 years has helped. I never, and I mean never, go anywhere without my cameras. I don't leave the truck further than bow range without my pack (or weapon for that matter) and most of the time my cameras are on the seat of the truck, ready for action.

Now, you may not want to carry all the stuff I do, but here's a short list just to give you an idea of what I'm willing to do to make sure I preserve memories.

I have two camera bodies, Canon 20Ds, which are digital SLR cameras. The 8.5 megapixel sensor is excellent and has all the resolution I'll ever need for great photos. More megapixels are probably overkill and files are so large you'll run into storage problems. I always set my cameras to the largest "superfine" format and use 2 Gig memory cards so I can shoot at will. You never know when you'll get the shot of a lifetime, and there usually isn't time to change the setting, even if you do remember.

On one of my bodies I have a wide-angle Canon 17 to 40mm L lens, and the other is armed with Canon's 100-400mm L telephoto lens. Because the sensors on my cameras have a 1.6 multiplier, these lenses, when compared to a standard film camera, are equivalent to 27-64 mm and 160-640mm. That's plenty of reach, and my long lens has image stabilization, so I can get serviceable handheld images provided the light is good.

My camera gear also includes my ever-present pack tripod, a 580EX flash, which I use extensively while taking "grip-and-grin" photos, a Canon Timer Remote Controller, extra batteries, and memory cards. Again, this is overkill for most bowhunters, but it shows how important photos are to both my work and my memories.

Point-and-shoot digital cameras have come a long way in recent years, and some of these tiny, easy to pack cameras are capable of taking very good photos of your experiences. They are so compact and easy to use there's absolutely no excuse to not have one in your pack at all times.

One negative of these cameras is shutter release speed, which is typically very slow. This is why some trail cameras miss so many deer. The shutter on an SLR camera is just as fast as a film camera, so I never miss a shot because of the delay. If you've tried to take photos of your active kids on Christmas morning with a point-and-shoot camera, you understand the dilemma.

While still cameras are the standard for preserving hunt memories, many hunters have gone to carrying camcorders in the field, trying to get footage of their hunting experiences. Personally, I avoid this habit, because I must get still images and that doesn't happen if I'm messing with a camcorder. But that's just me.

I did take a small camcorder that uses the mini DVD discs on a trip to Africa. It worked great, and the footage was easy to

This is the primary camera gear I take with me everywhere I go. It's overkill for most bowhunters. Even if you just stuff a point-and-shoot camera like the one in the middle in your pack and keep it there, I'll be happy. And you will too.

import into my computer and create a movie, much like television producers put together TV footage. If you have a major expedition planned, get movie-making software and experiment with it before you go. That will give you some idea about the support footage you'll need once your hunt starts.

Taking good still photos and video requires forethought. Don't wait until the opportunity presents itself. Spontaneous photos of your experience can only happen if you have your camera handy and not buried in your pack. Keep it close at hand, and if you like what you see, such as a sunset or your youngster in full camo face paint, you'll be more likely to preserve that memory if you don't have to go through all sorts of gyrations to get your camera out.

GRIP-AND-GRIN PHOTOS

For many hunters, grip-and-grin photos are very important. Sadly, to some, they aren't so important, which is why we see so many dead bucks on garage floors or in pickup boxes. Take for example, one world-class nontypical whitetail taken by a hunter in Ohio. The only image I've ever seen of that buck was in the back of a pickup.

Taking good kill photos is a skill that must be honed. The most important factor is time. For reasons I've never understood, everyone gets in a hurry after a kill.

Unless you're in grizzly country with no firearm and it's dark, take your time. Tell your hunting buddies or your guide to chill, because this is going to take time to do right. I usually warn my compatriots in advance that when I make a kill they're looking at a minimum of one hour, possibly two, just to get decent photos. If it's dark, I'll take some photos and then, if possible, wait until the next day to get daylight photos. Obviously, that's not always possible, especially in warm weather or when dealing with large animals like elk and moose.

The first thing I do after tagging the animal is look around for a good place to take my photos. The kill site is often in thick brush, and there's usually some blood around. I can appreciate the opinion of some who don't believe they should have to eliminate blood from their photos, but I disagree. Unless you're the only person who will ever see your photos, consider those who will. Death is never pretty, but you can do your best to show respect for the fallen animal and for those who will view your handiwork. If I can't eliminate any and all blood from my photos, I take it out later with Photoshop.

For my photo session I look for a place that will highlight the animal. After all, it is the star, not me. If you're dealing with antlers or horns, try to silhouette them against the sky (see Quick Tips for more thoughts). To do that you'll need to find a place where the sky is your background. Take the time to move your animal to the spot you want, even if that means loading it on an ATV and unloading it. A new location, with different light, often enhances the quality of your photos. Light is everything.

When it's time to take the grip-and-grin photos, make time to prepare the scene. Clip away vegetation that can reflect flash, brush the animal clean of debris, and make sure there are no signs of civilization (power lines, buildings, vehicles) in the background.

Once my spot is chosen, I position the animal in the most flattering way possible by choosing its best side, tucking the legs underneath, brushing its fur smooth, and removing all other objects that could distract the eye.

If you look in my pack, you'll always find some water and a Ziploc bag full of unscented baby wipes. Besides the obvious uses, these items are invaluable when it comes to cleaning up an animal before photos.

I immediately cut the tongue off deep in the throat so it doesn't flop out. Then I'll take wads of toilet paper and start stuffing them in the throat, nostrils, and wound to stop any leaking blood. You may start off with a clean animal, but moving it could cause bleeding you'll have to clean up.

I also carry a pair of glass eyes like those a taxidermist uses. They're half-circles, and you simply pop them under the eyelids and over the existing eyeball and posi-

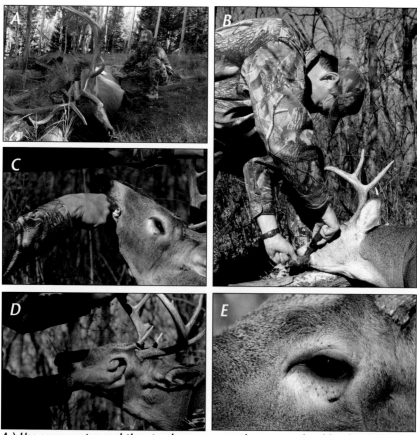

A.) Use some water and time to clean up wounds or any other blood. B.) Cut the tongue out first thing so you don't forget. C.) Stuff toilet paper into the throat and nostrils to prevent further draining. D.) Keep a pair of glass eyes in your pack and insert them under the eyelids. E.) Glass eyes give your animal life and prevent flash reflection.

tion them so they look natural. This does two things. It eliminates the "green eye" effect caused by your camera's flash reflecting off the animal's retina and covers up that cloudy eye look common to a dead animal. Glass eyes make your gorgeous critter look like it's about to get up and take off running.

QUICK TIPS

- Always take photos as if film is free, and in the case of digital, it is — kinda. You can go in and delete images you don't like later after reviewing them, but you can't delete or save photos you don't have. The difference between a great photo and garbage can be a blink.

- A tripod is essential if you're hunting alone, even if it's just a tiny six-inch model. Set up the photo with the tripod and then set your timer. It may require a bunch of trips back and forth, but keep shooting. I have a timer for my camera and can set the delay, the number of images, and the interval. That allows me to pose the animal like a body builder and let the camera work.

- Usually you'll have a buddy or a guide to help with the photos. Ask them to be patient, and direct them on how you want the photos to be taken. Review the images frequently so you know they're getting what you want.

- Never take grip-and-grin photos from a position above the hunter and animal. Always get at least level, but preferably lower than the subject. The idea is to make the animal look as good as possible, and lower angles always make antlers, horns, and heads look bigger.

- I hate photos where the animal's mouth is hanging open. To solve this I started carrying a surgeon's "towel clamp." I open the animal's mouth and with the sharp

A New Zealand red stag photo taken just as the sun went down. This image required a strong flash.

tips poked into the gum line, I clamp the jaws together. I leave the clamp on while I do other preparatory work and usually the jaw stiffens up in that position in a short time.

- Use fill flash on almost every grip-and-grin photograph you take. The flash fills in shadows, such as under cap brims, enhances colors, and just makes the image "pop." If you have good light, especially warm, low-angle light at either end of the day, take a few shots without flash.

- Be careful that a background of trees and brush doesn't blend in with antlers and diminish their impressiveness. Flash will highlight the antlers and make them stand out.

- On a sunny day, in the deep woods, the shadows of trees can be very harsh and always look darker in photos than to your eyes. This can be very distracting, so move your animal into either full sun or full shade, and take your photos in more consistent light.

- It's common to end up with a bloody arrow in your quiver. Take it out for the photo session, but be sure to put it in a safe place and don't forget it.

- There's a good chance you'll have bloody hands as well. Clean them up with baby wipes, creek water, or snow. Eliminate any and all blood, because the flash will highlight it, and you're not the only one who will see your images.

- Be very mindful of any shoots of grass or small plants in front of the camera and your animal. When using flash, especially at night, these annoying bits of vegetation will overexpose and dominate the photo. Remove anything that can reflect your flash.

I spent considerable time cleaning up this Burchell's Zebra taken in Namibia.

- Be careful how you hold the animal's head up. Grabbing it by the throat or jaw makes the face look distorted, or like you're strangling the life out of it. Large heads can get heavy, so time your pose with your photographer and tell him to shoot like crazy.

- If you choose to photograph your animal's antlers/horns and

Having the lake in the background adds a nice touch, but flash is a necessity because the camera will meter the bright sky. Without flash this would be a silhouette.

yourself against the sky, you must use flash on your camera. Otherwise your camera will meter for the brighter background and the subjects in the foreground will be dark, possibly even silhouetted.

• The number one mistake I see is the photographer not getting close enough or leaving far too much foreground in the photo. We don't want to see the ground. Get up very tight so the animal looks like it's kneeling on the bottom of the photo. Leave very little space on either side of the animal and only a little bit above the hunter's head (hopefully it's yours).

• The animal, and you, are the subjects, so eliminate all other distractions. Check the background for power lines, buildings, towers, and vehicles. I always try to eliminate civilization from any photo.

• Treat the animal with respect by making it look as good as possible, and do not commit the cardinal sin of sitting on the animal. It's the ultimate insult.

• Change up your photos by having the hunter look admiringly at the animal or its antlers. Change angles and get in different positions. Take some with your bow and some without. Take off a layer of clothing or even a hat. When you think you have enough angles and poses, do a few more. You'll never get the chance to do it over with that animal.

• Always take lots of vertical images. Turn your camera sideways and get up close. Crowd the edges of your viewfinder, but don't cut off heads, shoulders, antlers, and horns.

• Don't forget to include your hunting buddies or guide. Get them in for a few shots. More than likely they helped you take the animal in some way. Offer them copies of photos.

• Always review your photos as you go, just in case you notice a zipper open, dirt on your face, or a tongue hanging out.

Check for good exposure, then look the entire image over for things that are out of place. If you wait until you're done and back in camp, you won't be taking advantage of the greatest benefit of digital photography—instant evaluation.

- Once the grip-and-grin shots are over, take photos of the post-kill process, such as field-dressing, packing, dragging, and hauling. If there are antlers on your back, take silhouette shots against a sunset.

- There are so many more things to watch for, but you get the idea. When the occasion warrants, capture lots of images. I take a ton of photographs, but I've never been satisfied and always wish I'd taken more.

Black bears are difficult to photograph because there is no definition. That didn't bother me as I posed behind my seven-foot Manitoba bruin.

THE ANIMAL

Preserving the memories of your hunt also involves the animal itself. Each hunter puts a different value on preserving the animals they kill, ranging from saving the antlers, horns, or skulls to paying for full-body mounts. It all depends on how much they want to spend and how much room they have for mounts. Those are individual considerations better left to the hunter. But there are other ways to preserve those memories.

Elk ivories (canine teeth in the upper jaw), bear claws, turkey beards, and other parts can be used in various ways. Many hunters use elk ivory in rings, and I have an arm guard with ivories as strap keepers. It is a prized possession I actually use on every hunt. I also have a set of ivories from a red stag I killed in New Zealand that'll end up in a ring someday.

I keep all my antlers and write the year and location inside the skull caps if they aren't mounted. I have a collection of turkey beards, shed antlers, and skins from various animals. Anything that can remind me of the treasured days spent in the outdoors is worth keeping.

Preserving your bowhunting memories requires effort, time, and yes, money. Those precious days in the field are fleeting and can never be replicated. Plan ahead, recognize the moment, slow down, and take your time savoring the experience. Then capture that excitement so you can share it with others and relive it another day.

The stronger the memories, the longer they'll last.

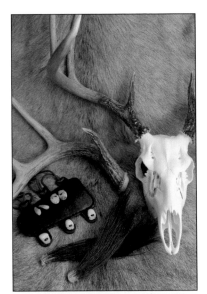

Parts of the animals you take with your bow are a piece of the adventure and will enhance your memories of days afield.

Epilogue

If you're an experienced bowhunter with a few years in your rearview mirror, you understand the commitment bowhunting demands. If you're a novice, you should have a better concept of that commitment after reading this book. Bowhunting isn't just a pastime or hobby. It's much more important than that.

As with anything in life, you can take bowhunting to whatever level you're comfortable with. I've been accused of being a bit too intense in some ways.

One example of that intensity is the length I will go to "make it happen." I have a favorite small patch of woods in Minnesota that's on the other side of a fast-flowing, four-foot-deep river. I used to wade it with chest waders but that was dangerous, and in November I always ended up having to put on frozen waders at the end of the hunt. When the river iced up I was done hunting that stand until I could walk on the ice.

Here's my solution to crossing a river that was always either too deep, too fast or half frozen. Maybe I do need therapy!

To solve this problem, I strung 150 feet of 8,000-pound-test steel cable across the river between two large trees. I designed a cable car with a bow rack and pulley system. Now, in the morning darkness, I can strap my bow on the rack, fasten my safety belt, and zip across the river suspended from the cable. I only make it to the bottom of the sag, then I have to use the pulley system to get to the other bank. I quietly slip 20 yards into my treestand and wait for the unsuspecting whitetails to come back from feeding. It has proven very effective, and I've taken some really good bucks on that property.

Not surprisingly, when I tell people that story they look at me as though I need therapy. That's quite possible, but to me, it's not quirky at all. It simply illustrates how much effort and intensity I put into my bowhunting. That commitment, over 27 years, has brought me to the conclusion of my first book, something I never envisioned when I flung my first arrow back in 1981.

Is it prerequisite to bellycrawl in the rain for three and a half hours or ride a cable across a river to be a successful bowhunter? Of course not. If you're content with bowhunting whitetails around home, be the best whitetail bowhunter you can be, realizing your level of commitment is often directly proportional to your level of success.

Your hunting attitude is also a fundamental piece of gear. Always approach your bowhunting with a positive outlook. Combine good equipment with thorough preparation, and your confidence will be strong enough to generate that positive attitude.

Anyone who has ever hunted with me has heard me say, "It's not a matter of if we fill our tags, just when and how big."

I don't intend those words to come off as cocky, but that's the attitude I carry in my mental backpack. Until the sun sets on the last day of my hunt, I always believe I can make it happen. Sometimes I'm wrong, sometimes not.

If this book plays even a small part in helping you become a more competent, committed, and confident bowhunter, I will have accomplished my goal.

Finally, I would ask you to pass it on. Take a youngster bowhunting. Mentor them. Teach them about the animals, about nature, about ethics, and about the circle of life. It's the single most significant thing you can do to perpetuate bowhunting.

Good luck and thanks so very much for your valuable time!

Both my sons are bowhunters, and now I'm working on my grandsons, Carson and Easton. Here, Carson and I enjoy his first day in the woods with his new bow. Hopefully there will be many, many more. Pass it on.

MANUFACTURERS CONTACT LIST

By Curt Wells

AAE, 938-772-9887, www.arizonaarchery.com

API Outdoors, 800-228-4846, www.apioutdoors.com

Alpine Archery, 208-746-4717, www.alpinearchery.com

Ameristep, Inc., 810-686-4035, www.ameristep.com

Archery Innovations (Anchor Sight), 218-563-2800, www.archeryinnovations.com

Arctic Shield, BKK Enterprises, 807-937-4377, www.bkkenterprises.com

Arizona Rim Country Products, 480-961-7995, www.ezfletch.com

ASAT Outdoors, LLC, 406-563-9336, www.asatcamo.com

Badlands Backpacks, 801-978-2207, www.badlandspacks.com

Balcom Bow Sling, see - Schaffer Performance Archery

Bass Pro Shops, 800-920-4400, www.basspro.com

Beman, 801-539-1400, www.beman.com/

Big Game Treestands, www.biggametreestands.com

Bitzenburger Machine & Tool, Inc., 888-724-5697, www.bitzenburger.com

Black's Creek Guide Gear, 800-742-1405, www.blacks-creek.com

Black Widow Bows, 417-725-3113, www.blackwidowbows.com

Bogen Tripods – check out www.bhphotovideo.com/

The Bohning Co. Ltd., 800-253-0136, www.bohning.com

BowFit LLC, 888-757-5541, www.bowfit.com/

BowJax, Inc., 208-762-3692, www.bowjax.com/

Bowmaster, Prototech Ind. Inc., 800-523-3109, www.prototechind.com

BowTech – 541-284-4711, www.bowtecharchery.com

Browning Archery, 520-838-2000, www.browning-archery.com

Buck Bomb, 866-850-6653, www.buckbomb.com

Buck Wing Products, Inc., 610-264-1122, www.buckwing.com

Burris Optics – 970-356-1670, www.burrisoptics.com

Bushnell Performance Optics – 800-423-3537, www.bushnell.com

Cabela's, 800-237-4444, www.cabelas.com

Canon USA, 800-652-2666, www.usa.canon.com

Carbon Express, 800-241-4833, www.carbonexpressarrows.com

Carol Davis Sportswear, 501-835-6331, www.cdsportswear.com

Carolina Archery Products – see Trophy Ridge

Carry-Lite Decoys, EBSCO Industries, 205-991-6600, www.carrylitedecoys.com

Carter Enterprises, 208-624-3467, www.carterenterprises.com

Catquiver, 800-240-2094, www.ranchosafari.com

Cherry Hill Outdoors, 724-588-0113, www.cherryhilloutdoors.com

CirCut Archery, 215-324-1000, www.circutcorp.com

Cobra Manufacturing, 800-352-6272, http://cobraarchery.com

Columbia Sportswear Co., www.columbia.com

Crooked Horn Outfitters, 877-722-5872, www.crookedhorn.com

Cuddeback, Non Typical Inc., 715-762-2260, www.cuddebackdigital.com

Cyclops Solutions, LLC, 877-269-8490, www.cyclopssolutions.com

Darton Archery – 989-728-4231, www.dartonarchery.com

Day One Camouflage, 800-347-2979, www.dayonecamouflage.com

Delta Sports Products, LLC, 800-708-0673, www.deltatargets.com

Doinker, Leven Industries, 818-700-2899, www.doinker.com

Doskocil – see Plano

Double Take Archery, 210-722-3484, www.doubletakearchery.com

Easton Technical Products, 801-539-1400, www.eastonarchery.com

Easy-Eye Archery Products, Inc., 888-908-7446, http://eze-eye.com

Eberlestock USA, LLC, 877-866-3047, www.eberlestock.com

Elimitrax, 334-677-7501, www.elimitraxboots.com

E.L.K. Inc., 800-272-4355, www.elkinc.com

Essential Gear, 800-582-3861, www.essentialgear.com

Falcon Products USA, (the Rattler), 949-929-6103, http://bowrattler.com

Fieldline, 800-438-3353, www.fieldline.com

Field Logic, Inc. 800-282-4868, www.fieldlogic.com

Flambeau, Inc., 800-232-3474, www.flambeauoutdoors.com

Jim Fletcher Archery, 760-379-2589, www.fletcherarchery.com

Fuse Archery, 801-363-2990, www.fusearchery.com

G5 Outdoors, 866-456-8836, http://g5outdoors.com

GSM-Walker Products, LLC, 877-269-8490, www.walkersgameear.com

Game Plan Gear, Inc., 877-544-6611, www.gameplangear.com/

Garmin, 800-800-1020, www.garmin.com

GerberGear, 800-950-6161, www.gerbergear.com

Gitzo, www.gitzo.com

Gold Tip, Inc., 801-229-1666, www.goldtip.com

Gorilla Treestands, 877-685-7817, www.gorillatreestands.com/

Gray Wolf Woolens, 715-623-5539, www.graywolfwoolens.com

Grim Reaper Broadheads, 877-474-6732, www.grimreaperbroadheads.com

Grizzly Treestands – see Ameristep

Heater Body Suit, 888-565-2652, www.heaterbodysuit.com

Hind Sight, Inc., 734-878-2842, www.hindsightco.com

Hip Clip, Third Hand Archery Accessories, 800-339-0232, www.thirdhandarchery.com

Hoyt USA – 801-363-2990, www.hoyt.com

Vertical By Horton, 800-551-7468, www.verticalbyhorton.com

Hunter Safety System, 256-773-7732, www.huntersafetysystem.com

Hunter's Specialties, 319-395-0321, www.hunterspec.com

Icebreaker Products, 800-343-2668, www.icebreakerinc.com

Inglewing C-Peep, visit www.keystonecountrystore.com

Justin Charles, 608-269-9665, www.justincharles.com

KA-BAR Knives, Inc., 800-282-0130, www.kabar.com

Kamik, www.kamik.com

Kifaru International, 800-222-6139, www.kifaru.com

King Of The Mountain, Inc., 970-962-9306, www.kingofthemountain.com

Knight and Hale, EBSCO Industries, 205-991-6600, www.knightandhale.com

Kwikee Kwiver, 800-346-7001, www.kwikeekwiver.com

L.L. Bean, 800-441-5713, www.llbean.com

LaCrosse Footwear, Inc., 800-323-2668, www.lacrossefootwear.com

Lakewood Products, 800-872-8458, www.lakewoodproducts.com

Leaf River Outdoor Products, 866-775-5351, www.myleafriver.com

Leatherman Tool Group, Inc. 800-847-8665, www.leatherman.com

Leica, 800-222-0118, www.leica-camera.us/hunting_optics/

Leupold & Stevens, 503-526-1400, www.leupold.com

Limbsaver, 360-427-6031, www.limbsaver.com

Loggy Bayou, 870-881-9778, www.loggybayou.com

Lowa Boots, 888-335-5692, www.lowaboots.com

Lowrance Electronics, 800-324-1356, www.lowrance.com

Lumenok, Burt Coyote Co, 309-358-1602, www.lumenok.net/

Magellan, Next Destination, www.magellan.com

Mag Instrument, Inc., 909-947-1006, www.maglite.com

Magnus, Inc., 620-793-9222, www.magnusbroadheads.com

Martin Archery, 509-529-2554, www.martinarchery.com

Mathews Solocam, 608-269-2728, www.mathewsinc.com

McKenzie Targets, see Delta Sports Products, www.mckenzie3d.com

MeanV Archery, 618-380-4012, www.meanvarchery.com

Meindl Boots, www.meindl.de/english

Montana Decoy Inc., 888-332-6998, www.montanadecoy.com

Morrell Manufacturing, Inc., 479-632-5622, www.morrelltargets.com

Mossy Oak Apparel, 800-331-5624, www.mossyoakapparel.com

Moultrie Feeders, 800-653-3334, www.moultriefeeders.com

Muck Boots, 877-438-6825, www.muckbootcompany.com

Muzzy Products Corp., 770-387-9300, www.muzzy.com

New Archery Products, 800-323-1279, http://newarchery.com/

Nikon USA, 800-645-6687, www.nikonusa.com

Nontypical Treestands – see Ameristep

Norway Industries, 800-778-4755, www.duravanes.com

Petzl America, 801-926-1500, www.petzl.com

Plano Molding, 800-226-9868, www.planomolding.com

Predator's View Peep Sight, 717-433-7126, www.predatorsviewpeepsight.com

Primos Hunting Calls, 800-523-2395, www.primos.com

Princeton Tec, 609-298-9331, www.princetontec.com

PSE Archery – 520-884-9065, www.pse-archery.com

QAD, Quality Archery Designs, 434-846-5839, www.qadinc.com

Quaker Boy Game Calls, 800-544-1600, wwwquakerboygamecalls.com

Rage Broadheads, 888-779-0092, www.ragebroadheads.com

Ram Products, 208-882-1396, www.ram-products.com

Really Right Stuff, 888-777-5557, www.reallyrightstuff.com

Realtree, www.realtree.com

Renzo's Decoys, 800-583-5416, www.renzosdecoys.com

Ripcord Arrow Rest, 406-683-0100, www.ripcordarrowrest.com

Rinehart Targets, 608-757-8153, www.rinehart3d.com

River's Edge Treestands, 800-450-3343, www.ardisam.com

Rocket Aeroheads – see Trophy Ridge

Rocky Mountain Broadheads, 715-395-0533, www.rockymtbroadheads.com

SKB Sports, 800-654-5992, www.skbcases.com

STS Archery, 731-286-6889, www.stsarchery.com

Sagen Saw, 701-873-5065, www.sageninc.com

Schaffer Performance Archery, 952-894-6169, www.schafferarchery.com

Schurz-a-Peep – see www.keystonecountrystore.com

Sims Vibration Labs – see Limbsaver

Sitka Gear, 877-748-5264, www.sitkagear.com

Sportsman's Outdoor Products, 801-562-8712, www.sophuntinggear.com

Spot-Hogg, 888-302-7768, http://spot-hogg.com/

Sleeping Indian Designs, Inc., 800-334-5457, www.woolcamo.com

Slick Trick, 870-934-0131, www.slicktrick.net

Slik Tripods, www.slik.com/

Stealth Archery, 402-304-1899, www.stealtharchery.com/

StealthCam, LLC, 888-304-6125, www.stealthcam.com

String Splitter, Sterner Duttera, 717-699-0005, www.sternerduttera.com

Stone Mountain Bow Strings, 208-476-7811, www.stonemountainbowstrings.com

Summit Treestands, 256-353-0634, www.summitstands.com

Surefire, LLC, 800-828-8809, www.surefire.com

Swarovski Optik – 401-734-1800, www.swarovskioptik.com

3River's Archery, 888-329-9872, www.3riversarchery.com

ThermaCELL, Schawbel Corp., 866-753-3837, www.mosquitorepellent.com

Tight Point, Shuttle T-Lock, 877-878-5625, www.tightpoint.com

Timberline Archery Products, 800-434-2708, www.timberline-archery.com

Tim's Archery Goat Tuff Glue – see www.keystonecountrystore.com

Trophy Ridge, 800-694-9494, www.trophyridge.com

Trophy Taker, Inc., 406-826-0602, www.trophytaker.com

T.R.U. Ball Release, 434-929-2800, www.truball.com/

Tru-Fire, 920-923-6866, www.trufire.com

TRUGLO, 972-774-0300, http://truglo.com

Wayne Carlton Calls – see Hunter's Specialties

Wiggy's Inc., 866-411-6465, www.wiggys.com/

Wilderness Sound Productions, Jones Calls, 800-437-0006, www.jonescalls.com

Wildlife Research Center, 800-873-5873, www.wildlife.com

Winner's Choice Custom Bowstrings, 541-575-0818, www.winnerschoicestrings.com

Wolverine Boots, 866-699-7369, www.wolverine.com

Wyoming Saw, Wyoming Knife, 970-224-3454, www.wyomingknife.com

Under Armour, 888-727-6687, www.underarmour.com

Vanguard USA Inc., 800-875-3322, www.vanguardusa.com

Vapor Trail Archery, 800-310-8110, www.vaportrailarchery.com

Vibracheck Products – see PSE Archery

Vital Gear, 859-253-1003, www.vitalgear.net

Vortex Optics, 800-426-0048, www.vortexoptics.com

Zeiss Sport Optics, 800-441-3005, www.zeiss.com/sports

Zwickey Broadheads – see 3Rivers Archery, www.3riversarchery.com

GLOSSARY OF TERMS

actuator cord - Cord that attaches to down buss cable or cable slide that lifts a drop-away rest to the up position, then allows it to fall away.

adhesive fleece - Soft material with sticky tape on back to be applied to many surfaces to quiet noise.

anchor point - A precise and consistent position of the hand, release, and bowstring at full draw.

arm guard - A device worn on the bow arm that protects if from string slap and/or keeps bulky clothing out of the way of the bowstring.

arrow gripper - The section of a quiver that holds the arrow shafts, typically a slot in rubber material.

arrow insert - A lightweight aluminum tube with female threads that slips inside an arrow shaft and accepts the threads of a field tip or broadhead.

arrow level - Small level with a spring clamp that can be attached to an arrow shaft.

arrow rest - Device that attaches to bow riser and holds arrow shaft in place as it is drawn and released.

arrow wrap - Thin adhesive wrap applied to back end of arrow for visibility and enhanced glue adhesion for feathers or vanes.

axle-to-axle length - Precise distance, in inches, between the axles on a compound bow.

back-tension release - A mechanical release designed to fire only after the correct amount of tension is applied to the back muscles while at full draw.

bivouac - Term applied to a type of hunt that involves packing all gear deep into the wilderness and staying for an extended period of time.

bowstring - Primary string connecting the limbs and/or eccentrics of a bow. The arrow is clipped to the bowstring.

bow vise - This device clamps to a table top and securely holds a bow during maintenance.

brace height - The distance in inches from the bowstring to the deepest throat of the grip.

broadhead - An arrow tip fitted with ultra-sharp blades used for hunting.

buss cable - On compound bows, the buss cable is the string that extends from connection points on the limb or eccentrics, providing the geometry for let off.

cable guard - A rod that extends from the riser rearward, holding the buss cables out of the arrow's line of flight.

cable guard slide - This device, often made of Teflon, fits under the buss cables on a cable guard to reduce friction and wear.

cam - Otherwise known as an eccentric, the cam is the round or oval "wheel" at each end of a compound bow.

capture rest - A rest designed to capture the arrow during the shot sequence, preventing the arrow from falling off the rest.

carbon arrow - An arrow constructed of carbon fibers, often in sheets and rolled into an arrow shaft. Some designs are woven or wrapped.

centershot - A precise point, usually determined at the arrow rest, that is directly in line with the travel of the released bowstring.

chronograph - An electronic device that measures arrow speed in feet-per-second.

cock feather/vane - Usually one of three vanes or feathers that's a different color to aid in the correct orientation of the arrow on the bowstring.

creep - Creep is the unrecoverable elongation of a bowstring or buss cable. It takes place over time and many shots and is less of a problem in custom-made strings.

cresting - Either paint or arrow wraps applied to the back portion of an arrow shaft for enhanced visibility, fletching adhesion, or simply for a custom look.

cut diameter - The measurement in inches of the maximum cut width of a broadhead.

cut-on-contact broadhead - Broadhead design with a tip that is sharpened to a fine edge, extending rearward like a sword tip.

deflex - Refers to a bow riser design in which the grip section is forward of the limb bolts.

dovetail mount - Two-part mounting device for a bowsight that can be quickly removed.

draw cycle - Term given to the "feel" of a compound bow as it's drawn. The point of heaviest draw weight, the let off, and the valley occur in different parts of the draw cycle on different bows. Each cam design has its own feel.

draw length - The critical distance, in inches, from the deepest throat of the grip to the archer's anchor point.

drop-away rest - An arrow rest designed to drop downward within microseconds after the arrow is released. It should offer total fletching clearance and excellent flight.

dry fire - The act of drawing and releasing a bow without an arrow on the string. Almost always results in damage to the bow.

feather - A cut turkey feather attached to the rear of an arrow to provide stability.

feet-per-second - Measurement of the speed of an arrow in flight.

ferrule - The body section of a broadhead into which the blades are inserted.

fiber optic - Plastic fibers that gather light and concentrate it at the tip for a sight's pin or aiming point.

field tip - Tip for an arrow, typically the same diameter, used for target practice.

finger glove - A three-fingered glove used by archers who release the string with fingers.

finger pinch - Term used when the angle of the bowstring at full draw pinches the archer's fingers. The shorter the bow, the more finger pinch.

finger tab - Alternative to a finger glove, this leather tab provides a slick surface between the bowstring and the archer's fingers.

fixed-blade broadhead - A broadhead with blades that do not move upon impact.

fletching - Term given to either feathers or vanes, typically three, attached to the rear of an arrow to provide rotation and stabilization.

fletching jig - Device used to glue vanes or feathers to an arrow shaft.

force draw curve - A graph that illustrates the power stroke of a bow, showing the peak draw weight, the letoff, and where they occur in the draw cycle.

forgiveness - Term given to a bow describing its ease of use. A forgiving bow is accurate despite less-than-perfect form by the archer.

front of center/FOC - An arrow must be front-heavy, and FOC describes the percent of the arrow's weight that is forward of the center balance point.

grain - Unit of measurement applied to all parts of arrows, broadheads, etc.

grip - That part of a bow's riser that the archer holds in his bow hand.

hand shock - Term given to the amount of recoil felt by the archer at the moment of release.

hang-on treestand - Treestand that is portable and can be "hung" from most trees.

helical - The orientation of a vane or feather that twists slightly around an arrow shaft with the purpose of imparting rotation.

idler wheel - The simple round wheel at the top of a single-cam bow.

instinctive shooting - The art of shooting bow and arrow without sight pins.

kick-out - Term given when the blades of a mechanical broadhead kick the arrow outward when the target is hit at a sharp angle.

kinetic energy - A description of energy in foot pounds often used to determine potential penetration of an arrow of specific weight at a specific speed.

launcher - That part of an arrow rest that supports the arrow shaft.

LED - Light Emitting Diode encased in a resin and used in flashlights and head-lamps.

letoff - A description of the reduction in draw weight that occurs as the eccentrics on a compound bow "roll over."

lighted nock - Electronic device inside a plastic arrow nock that lights up upon release, aiding the archer in determining arrow impact, and in recovering the arrow.

limb bolts - Heavy bolts at the front end of the bow's limbs that secure the limbs to the riser and allow the adjustment of draw weight.

limb dampener - Device, usually some type of rubber or polymer, attached to the bow's limbs and intended to soak up vibration.

longbow - Traditional bow design with long, straight geometry.

mass weight - The weight of a bow, usually stated before the addition of accessories.

mechanical broadhead - A broadhead with low-profile blades designed to open on impact.

mechanical release - A handheld device that clips to the bowstring and allows for a cleaner release when a trigger is pulled.

micro-adjust - Description of an enhanced bowsight or rest design that can be adjusted in small amounts. A graduated scale usually aids in that adjustment.

module - Some cam designs employ modules that determine draw length. By switching modules you can adjust the draw length of some bows.

momentum - The measurement of the continuation of force of a body such as an arrow shaft.

nock - A plastic device inserted into the rear end of an arrow shaft that is split to accept the bowstring.

nock travel - Term given to the path of travel the arrow nock takes during the launch. "Straight and level" is perfect but not always achievable with some bow designs.

objective lens - The large lens on the far end of a binocular or spotting scope.

offset - Term given to a feather or vane orientation that is offset several degrees at the front and rear of the fletching to create rotation in the flight of the arrow.

paper tune - Procedure where the archer stands six to eight feet in front of a piece of paper suspended in front of a backstop. As the archer shoots, adjustments are made until the arrow flies through the paper perfectly, with the nock directly behind the tip, creating a "bullet hole."

parabolic cut - a feather or vane that's cut with a rounded taper on the back end.

parallel limbs - Bow design with the limbs at or near parallel to each other at full draw. At the shot, the force of the opposing limbs cancel each other and reduce hand shock.

peep sight - Small circular device inserted in the bowstring and used as a rear reference point. The archer looks through the peep and aligns the sight pin on the target.

point of impact - The exact spot of the arrow's impact on a target or animal.

porro prism - An older binocular design that bounces the view off mirrors creating a bulkier binocular.

power stroke - The distance that an arrow is under the influence of the bow-string. It's typically measured from the string at rest to full draw.

press - Mechanical device that serves to compress a bow's limbs, relaxing the string and cables so maintenance can be performed.

recurve - Traditional bow design that includes limbs that curve toward the archer then back, providing enhanced arrow speed as opposed to a longbow.

reflex - A reflex design in a bow's riser means the grip section is rearward of the limb bolt section. The degree of reflex varies from bow to bow.

replaceable-blade broadhead - Broadhead with removable blades that can be easily replaced with new, sharp blades.

riser - The main handle section of a bow with limb pockets at each end — a shelf and a grip section.

roof prism - Binocular design in which the barrels are in-line. Superior design that reduces weight and bulk.

roller guard - Improved version of a cable guard in that it incorporates rollers rather than slides to reduce friction.

selection chart - Arrow selection charts help the archer choose the correctly spined arrow shaft by referencing draw weight, arrow length, and other factors.

serving thread - Heavy duty thread used to wrap around the bowstring, providing a secure point of connection for the arrow nock, among other uses.

shaft - Term used to describe an arrow shaft before fletching is attached.

shelf - That part of a bow's riser just above the grip where the arrow rest is attached.

shield cut - The cut design on a feather or vane that includes a "corner" on the back.

shoot-through rest - An older style rest, still used by some archers, that does not drop away. Consists of two prongs and the cock vane or feather shoots through the prongs.

sight guard - The round or oval metallic guard that encircles and protects the pins on a bowsight.

sight pin - Small pin, usually tipped with a fiber optic, used as an aiming point that can be adjusted for both windage and elevation.

slave cable - Cable in some cam designs, such as a binary cam, that connects the two eccentrics and maintains synchronization.

solid limb - bow limb design that is solid with a split at the end to accept the cam.

spine - The degree of deflection a particular arrow shaft has. A measure of stiffness.

split harness - A buss cable that is split at one end and attaches to the outer axles of the cams.

split limb - Bow limb design with two completely separate limb sections and a space in between.

stabilizer - Device attached to the front of the bow's riser to help reduce shock and vibration and provide balance.

static rest - An arrow rest that does not move at the shot. Opposite of a drop-away rest.

string level - Bubble level device that clips to the bowstring to make sure it is vertical when tuning and setting the arrow rest height.

string loop - Short piece of cord tied to the bowstring with two cow hitches. An alternative to a nocking point.

string silencer - Any piece of material, rubber, hair, etc. that is attached to the bowstring to absorb string oscillation and vibration.

string suppressor - A static device attached to the riser or limb that contacts the bowstring at rest. At the shot this device drastically reduces string oscillation.

synchronization - Describes the simultaneous rotation of the cams on a dual cam or hybrid cam bow. That rotation must occur at the same time

target panic - A common mental disorder that affects an archer's concentration and abilty to release the bowstring. A fear of missing.

thermals - The flow of air throughout different parts of a day that depends on the warming and cooling of air.

throat of the grip - The deepest part of the bow grip where the crotch between the thumb and forefinger makes contact.

torquing grip - The act of imparting twist or forceful pressure on a grip at full draw.

trigger lock tripod mount - A type of tripod head with a squeeze-grip trigger. You squeeze the grip to adjust the spotting scope then let go to lock.

tune - Refers to the act of combining the correct components and adjustments to a bow so that arrows fly well.

valley - The bottom of the draw cycle or the point of least draw weight at full let-off.

vane - A plastic version of the feather, required for the stabilization of the arrow.

vitals - Term used to describe the heart/lung region of a game animal.

wall - The point of full draw when a cam/eccentric comes to a full stop. Some cam designs have a "soft" wall, others a "hard" wall. Most of today's bows have hard walls.

waypoint - A term used to describe a specific location that is stored in a GPS unit and saved for further reference.

weight tubes - Thin plastic tubes that can be slipped into an arrow shaft to increase weight by two or three grains per inch.

NOTES